JANE AUSTEN

FACTS AND PROBLEMS

Oxford University Press, Amen House, London E.C. 4

GLASGOW NEW YORK TORONTO MELBOURNE WELLINGTON
BOMBAY CALCUTTA MADRAS CAPE TOWN

Geoffrey Cumberlege, Publisher to the University

L'aimable Jane.

See p. 214

JANE AUSTEN

FACTS AND PROBLEMS

THE CLARK LECTURES

Trinity College, Cambridge, 1948

by

R. W. CHAPMAN

Sometime Fellow of
Magdalen College, Oxford

OXFORD
AT THE CLARENDON PRESS

*'Of all great writers the most
difficult to catch in the act of
greatness.'*

VIRGINIA WOOLF

FIRST PUBLISHED DECEMBER 1948
REPRINTED JANUARY 1949

Reprinted lithographically in Great Britain at the
University Press, Oxford, 1950, by Charles Batey,
Printer to the University, from corrected sheets of
the first edition

PREFACE

THE scope of this little book perhaps admits a brief explanation. Though I have spent a substantial slice of my life in the company of Jane Austen, her family, her friends, and her fictions, I have had no impulse to attempt her life, or any systematic criticism of her art. Many years ago, however, I was moved to make a kind of survey that is neither the one nor the other. Its design is indicated by my title, which follows, at a respectful distance, the work of a greater scholar on a mightier theme: Sir Edmund Chambers on Shakespeare. But the encouragement of my friends failed to bring me to the point of publication, or even of necessary revision. The needed stimulus was not applied until the Council of Trinity College, Cambridge, honoured me by appointment as Clark Lecturer.

Grateful acknowledgement is due to those critics, kindly but not unexacting, who have read my manuscript or my proofs or both—Mr. R. A. Austen Leigh, Lord David Cecil, Miss Elizabeth Jenkins, Miss Mary Lascelles, Miss A. L. Tallmadge, and my wife. The Syndics of the Cambridge University Press have generously allowed the book to come from another place, where it had long been pledged.

NOTE

A REPRINT enables me to make a few very slight improvements suggested by my friends.

October 1949   R. W. C.

CONTENTS

CONTENTS

I

JANE AUSTEN'S FAMILY

JANE AUSTEN never married, and most of her life was a part of the family life of three generations. Much of it was given to family service—as daughter and niece, as sister, as aunt. However her writing might absorb her, the family was her first and, I think, her dearest concern. She spent upon it the same talents, and the same affection, as she gave to the creatures of her fancy. The letters to which we owe almost all our knowledge of her life are family letters. One of her nieces, naturally enough, thought that for that reason the letters could not interest the public. Her opinion has been echoed by many indifferent readers of the letters, but not by those who are most in sympathy with their writer. Those who turn to the letters in the hope that they may ignore the commonplace of family life, and find rapid enlightenment on the novelist's character, or her way of work, will almost certainly be disappointed. Jane Austen shows a great deal of herself in her letters, but we cannot have it except on her own terms. And we cannot imagine that she would wish us to read them, unless we earn it by taking an interest in the people and the things she loved.

The terms are not onerous. The family and its connexions are attractive in themselves—a vigorous, versatile race—and the social scene which their lives make up is drawn by our observer with rare delicacy and skill. The social historian has at his command no equal picture of the life of the upper middle class in England in George the Third's last years.

The subject is best approached by reading and rereading the letters themselves, with some of the aids which have been variously supplied for their better comprehension. But an outline of it must be attempted here, because no account of Jane Austen is otherwise intelligible. The task is not easy; for the Austens and their relations by marriage were numerous and prolific; and their historian, labouring to be lucid, is embarrassed by their tendency to marry twice, and to change or amplify their surnames.

The Austens were by origin clothiers in Kent. Hasted, the eighteenth-century historian of the county, records that these clothiers were called 'the Gray Coats of Kent'. The phrase is quoted in a marginal note written by Jane Austen in one of the few books in her library that we know to have survived.[1] The Austens were men of substance in the neighbourhood of Sevenoaks in the sixteenth cen-

<hr />

[1] See p. 38.

tury, and their descendants are still landowners in that district.

Jane's father, George Austen (1731–1805), was the son of William Austen, a surgeon of Tonbridge, and Rebecca his wife, and was very early left an orphan. He was befriended by an uncle, Francis Austen, who sent him to Tonbridge School, whence he became a scholar of St. John's College, Oxford. He was later a Fellow of his College, and taking orders obtained in 1761 the living of Steventon in Hants, by presentation from his kinsman Thomas Knight of Godmersham (of whom more hereafter), and in 1773 the adjacent living of Deane, bought for him by his uncle Francis. 'This was no very gross case of plurality, according to the ideas of that time, for the two villages were little more than a mile apart, and their united populations scarcely amounted to three hundred.'[1] He lived at Steventon, married, and brought up a family; retired to Bath in 1801, and died there in 1805.

William Austen had married a widow, and most of our knowledge of George Austen's early married life comes from letters written by the Austens to George's half-brother William Walter and his wife. Otherwise the Walters do not much concern us, and the Austen family (of *this* generation) is simple, for

[1] *Memoir*, ch. 1.

William and Rebecca had only two children who matter, George and Philadelphia. Philadelphia, Mrs. Hancock, will bring us acquainted with Warren Hastings and, through her only daughter Eliza, with the French Revolution. But Jane Austen knew none of her grandparents, and her cousin Eliza (who was also her sister-in-law) was her only intimate on that side of the house.

It is, however, in the Austen pedigree that we trace the connexion with the Knights of Godmersham near Canterbury and of Chawton in Hants— the connexion which did more than anything else to determine Jane's course of life. Thomas Knight was connected with the Austens by marriage, and it was he who gave George Austen his living. His son, a second Thomas (d. 1794), married Catherine Knatchbull (1753–1812). Being childless, Mr. and Mrs. Knight made George Austen's third son Edward their heir. That is why Edward ultimately (in 1812) became Knight; 'I must learn', wrote his sister, 'to make a better K'; and Mrs. Knight's maiden name deserves notice, for Jane's favourite niece, Fanny Knight, married into that family and, as Lady Knatchbull, was the mother of the first editor of the letters.

Jane Austen's mother takes us into deeper waters. Cassandra Austen (1739–1827) was a Leigh of

Adlestrop in Gloucestershire; a younger, but ennobled, branch of the same family is Leigh of Stoneleigh in Warwickshire. Cassandra's grandfather had married a Brydges, and so became brother-in-law to the Duke of Chandos; some of his daughters were brought up in the splendours of Canons. Of Cassandra's uncles, the eldest was father and grandfather of two Leighs who, in Jane's own time, succeeded to the Stoneleigh estates; another was Theophilus Leigh, Master of Balliol. Her father, Thomas Leigh, was a Fellow of All Souls, and held the college living of Harpsden[1] near Henley.

Theophilus Leigh had a daughter Cassandra, who married Samuel Cooke, Vicar of Great Bookham in Surrey. Mr. Cooke was Jane's godfather, and his children George and Mary were among her early intimates.

Thomas Leigh had three children, James, Jane, and Cassandra. Jane married the Rev. Edward Cooper, and they had two children (*our* Jane's only first cousins on her mother's side), Edward and Jane. Edward married Caroline Lybbe Powys[2] and had a large family. But they lived in Staffordshire, and the Austens did not admire Edward's published sermons; relations were not very close. Jane

---

[1] J.A. spells it phonetically, *Harden*.
[2] See p. 169.

married Tom Williams, R.N., who became Admiral and Sir Thomas, which was interesting, but Jane unhappily was killed in an accident in 1798. Moreover, Jane's Aunt Jane, the elder Mrs. Cooper, died in 1783, and her husband in 1792. Consequently the terms 'My Uncle' and 'My Aunt' are applied, in the letters, exclusively and unambiguously to Mrs. Austen's only brother and his wife.

James Leigh, who long before Jane was born had become Leigh Perrot of Northleigh in Oxfordshire, died in the same year as his niece, 1817; his wife Jane Cholmeley lived to 1836. The Leigh Perrots were wealthy and childless; they lived partly in Bath, where the Austens sometimes paid them visits, partly at Scarlets in Berkshire. George Austen's eldest son James was looked on as his uncle's natural heir, but he died soon after him in 1819; his son James Edward inherited the property on his great-aunt's death, and became Austen Leigh in 1837.

It is when we come to Jane Austen's own generation that the canvas begins to be crowded; not with cousins, for them we have easily exhausted, but with sisters-in-law, nephews, and nieces. Jane Austen 'liked first cousins to be first cousins', but had not enough material to call forth her full cousinly powers. Of her wealth of interest and sympathy as a sister we have eloquent testimony. But she 'always maintained the importance of aunts'; and perhaps might have agreed that she shone most brightly as an aunt. There is something, in the role of the consummate aunt, not unlike her relation to those young people who owed their existence to her genius.

Six sons and two daughters were born at Steventon, all of whom survived their father. Five of the sons married nine wives and had issue.

James Austen (1765–1819) was no doubt so named in compliment to his mother's only brother. He was educated first by his father and then at St. John's College, Oxford—not because his father had been Fellow of that college, but because, through his mother, he was Founder's kin. He took orders, and had curacies at Overton, near Steventon, and at Deane. In 1792 he married Anne, daughter of General and Lady Jane Mathew; Lady Jane was a Bertie, daughter of the second Duke of Ancaster. Anne Austen died within three years of her marriage, leaving one daughter, who is the most interesting of all Jane Austen's nieces. Jane Anna Elizabeth's (1793–1872) plurality of names was perhaps a token of ducal ancestry; we should regard the Jane as being in her grandmother's honour, not her youthful aunt's.

James Austen married again in 1797. His second wife was Mary Lloyd, a clergyman's daughter. The

Lloyds, especially Mary and her sister Martha, are very important figures in the letters, as will be seen later. James and Mary (often 'Mrs. J.A.', to distinguish her from another sister-in-law and from other Marys) had two children. James Edward Austen (1798–1874) became as we have seen his great-uncle's heir, and was the founder of the distinguished family of Austen Leigh. His second name is that of his uncle and godfather Edward Austen. Caroline Mary Craven Austen (1805–80; I cannot account for Caroline, but her mother was connected with Lord Craven's family) never married. She is one of the chief sources of our knowledge of her aunt.

James Austen succeeded his father as rector, and lived quietly at Steventon until his death. While a Fellow of St. John's he had edited, and contributed to, a periodical of a type then familiar, *The Loiterer*. In this he had the help of his brother Henry. He was a man of reading and reflection; given to composition in verse[1] and prose—though not, since *The Loiterer*, to publication; and his son thought that he directed Jane's reading and formed her taste, much as Edmund Bertram did Fanny's. His health does

[1] He was almost certainly the author of the blank-verse description of Steventon by 'one who knew and loved it well', quoted in the *Memoir*; see my edition, note to p. 20.

not seem to have been very good, nor his temper always very happy. But he was undoubtedly, like his children and many of his descendants, a man of strong character.

The second son, George (1766–1838), is never mentioned in the extant letters. We are told that all the children were put out to nurse, and that one or both of their parents visited them every day.[1] A letter from Mrs. Austen quoted in the *Life*[2] shows that 'my poor little George' had fits, and evidently he was never able to take his place in the family. If he never learned to talk, might that explain Jane's knowledge of the dumb alphabet?[3]

The third son, Edward (1768–1852; Knight 1812), was born with a silver spoon in his mouth. It was not visible at birth, or he must have been called Thomas and not Edward (in compliment perhaps to his mother's brother-in-law Dr. Edward Cooper). He showed, his mother tells us, no pretensions to scholarship; but he became a good man of business. Fortunately he was never called on for anything but to be amiable and happy, and to make others happy; to be a generous son and brother, an indulgent father, and doubtless an easy landlord. He and his sister Cassandra may have been in Jane's mind when she described Charles Bingley and Jane

[1] *Life* 18.   [2] p. 20.   [3] Letter 62.

Bennet: 'so complying, that nothing will ever be resolved on; so easy, that every servant will cheat you; and so generous, that you will always exceed your income.'

As we have seen, Thomas Knight of Godmersham and Chawton, whose father was related to George Austen and gave him the living of Steventon, had no children. He owned most of Steventon parish, and as he never resided there he seems to have regarded George Austen as his representative; it was not unnatural that he should turn to him for an heir. It was also natural, perhaps, that Edward should be thought of, since James was likely to be otherwise endowed. But it is certain that Mr. and Mrs. Knight took a fancy to the boy. Family tradition[1] records that when a visit was proposed Edward's father had scruples about the Latin grammar; but Mrs. Austen decided it: 'I think, my dear, you had better oblige your cousins and let the child go.' He became in due course the adopted son and heir, and after a grand tour was suitably married. His bride was Elizabeth, daughter of Sir Brook Bridges, baronet of Goodnestone. Goodnestone is pronounced Gunston, and like Godmersham is near Canterbury. The young couple lived for a time at Rowling, a Bridges house, but before long moved

[1] *Life* 48.

to Godmersham, the widowed Mrs. Knight choosing to vacate her house and surrender her fortune, and to retire to Canterbury with an annuity. Details of this happy family compact are printed in the *Life*.[1] Edward's sisters began to visit him soon after his marriage, first at Rowling, later at Godmersham. Moreover, Lady Bridges, a benevolent and dominating widow, lived with unmarried daughters at Goodnestone Farm. Goodnestone Farm is not a farm, but a good house within a stone's throw of the Great House. Lady Bridges's benevolence extended to her son-in-law's family, and so we have Godmersham–Goodnestone letters, exchanged by our sisters when they were both in East Kent. It will be convenient to note the distinction (though J.A. does not always observe it) between Bridges and Brydges; for another Kentish family, that of Sir Egerton Brydges, will come into the picture later.

The Edward Austens had many children, before the young wife died after the birth of the last. Some readers of the *Letters* will learn to know them all, as well as their numerous Bridges uncles and aunts, and *their* husbands and wives and children, and all the baronets' houses in which they visited. But for the present we need notice only one, the eldest,

[1] p. 74.

Jane's favourite niece. Fanny Catherine Austen
(Knight; 1793–1882) owed her names to her
mother's mother, Fanny Lady Bridges, and her
fairy godmother Mrs. Catherine (Thomas) Knight.
When her mother died in 1808 she took charge of
her father and his household, and did it so well that
Edward was contented with his widowhood and his
ten other children. She survived two love affairs,
in which she took counsel of her aunt, and did not
marry till 1820 when, as we have seen, she became
Lady Knatchbull.

Edward Austen lived mainly at Godmersham,
but he was also owner of Chawton in Hants, and it
was there that he settled his mother and sisters in
1809; a few years later he took to spending part of
each summer there, and filling the Great House and
the Cottage with young life.

The fourth son, Henry Thomas Austen (1771–
1850), was probably Thomas (Henry is obscure)
because his mother's father was Thomas Leigh.
Henry is known to have been Jane's favourite
brother, as Edward was Cassandra's. His character
and his life were calculated to sustain her interest,
though not always to promote her happiness. He
did and suffered unusual and unexpected things.
Like his brother James, he was educated by his
father and at St. John's; but though brilliantly clever

he did not win a fellowship or (until many years later) take orders. He had military ambitions, like James Boswell before him, and was actually Captain and Adjutant of the Oxford Militia. He seems to have engaged himself, at five-and-twenty, to a Miss Pearson.[1] A year later he married, in 1797, a lady ten years his senior, his cousin Eliza (1761–1813), the only daughter of George Austen's only sister Philadelphia.

Philadelphia Austen, being a penniless girl, was shipped to India, a common practice. There she duly made a not very prosperous marriage. Her husband was a surgeon at Fort St. David, named Hancock, and they had one daughter. For reasons which remain obscure, the infant Eliza's godfather was Warren Hastings. Hancock did not prosper, and Hastings eventually gave him £10,000 in trust for himself, his wife, and his daughter. The intimacy continued after the death of the parents, and ultimately gave us Hastings's opinion of *Pride and Prejudice*.

Eliza and her parents left India in 1764–5. Her father had soon to return for financial reasons; but his wife and daughter remained in Europe, partly in England, where they paid visits to Steventon, and partly in Paris, where Eliza married, in 1781, Jean

[1] See my index to the *Letters*, s.v. Pearson.

Capotte, Comte de Feuillide. She lost her mother in 1791–2 (her father had died in 1775), her husband (by the guillotine) in 1794, and her little boy Hastings in 1801.

So Henry Austen, at six-and-twenty, an officer in the militia, married his first cousin, the widow of a French aristocrat and the god-daughter of a Governor-General of India, encumbered with a little boy. His sanguine temperament probably found no difficulty in the situation,[1] and within a few years we find him living in Upper Berkeley Street, with an office in Cleveland Court. Not long afterwards they are in Brompton; Henry is now a banker in partnership with a brother officer named Maunde, and has an office in the Albany, and the firm of Austen, Maunde, and Tilson is in Henrietta Street, Covent Garden. He is prosperous, and becomes Receiver-General for Oxfordshire in 1813; his wife dies in that year, and he goes to live in Henrietta Street; within a year he is in Hans Place, and likely to marry again; two years later he is bankrupt in March, takes orders, and is curate of Bentley near Alton in December. 'His mind is not a mind for affliction.'[2]

Henry's character is enigmatical. The *Memoir*

[1] Eliza described him as 'in possession of a comfortable income'. *Life* 107.   [2] Letter 81.

gives a brief and guarded account of him; he 'had perhaps less steadiness of purpose than his brothers'. Anna, writing privately, is more outspoken; there were some 'who considered his abilities greater in show than in reality'. They agree that he was a brilliant talker; and Anna is guilty of brilliance herself when she writes that 'his hopefulness of temper, in adapting itself to all circumstances, even the adverse, seemed to create a perpetual sunshine'. His sister Jane, whose judgement partiality never blinded, vouches for his wit and his infectious gaiety; he could not 'help being amusing'; his arrival 'put life and wit into the party'. But this brilliance does not appear in such of his compositions as have been published. The authors of the *Life*, relying perhaps on more evidence than they print, describe his style as 'grandiloquent'.[1] The effusions they quote are youthful. The *Biographical Notice* of his sister is not pompous; but though it shows judgement and taste as well as good feeling, it cannot be called brilliant. Again, the imprudence, or bad luck, which ruined his own fortune, brought also heavy losses to his uncle and his brothers; and the invincible cheerfulness with which he bore it may have been trying. Yet he seems to have been quickly forgiven. He spent his remaining thirty-four years in the county

[1] *Life* 49, 79.

of his birth as a parish clergyman. His favourite sister heard him take duty at Chawton immediately after his ordination, and had owned to a friend that 'It will be a nervous hour for our pew, though we hear that he acquits himself with as much ease and collectedness, as if he had been used to it all his life'.[1] That does not surprise us; Henry Crawford would have done equally well; but Henry Austen, unlike his namesake, was content to do it 'for a constancy'. 'Uncle Henry writes very superior sermons', Jane tells her nephew;[2] and we know that she was a student of sermons;[3] his niece Anna conceded that he was an exemplary parish priest.

The series of sons is now interrupted by a daughter, and the rest of the family is symmetrically arranged, the two sailors alternating with the two sisters. The order is Cassandra, Frank, Jane, Charles. The elder daughter, Cassandra Elizabeth Austen (1773–1845), was named after her mother and her godmother, Miss (or 'Mrs.') Elizabeth Leigh of Adlestrop. In her early twenties she was engaged to the Rev. Thomas Fowle, who went to the West Indies as an army chaplain and died there. Cassandra lived with her mother and sister till Jane died in 1817, then with her mother till her death in

[1] Letter 139.   [2] Letter 134.
[3] Letter 101.

1827; later she lived alone at Chawton, but was much with her brother Frank at Portsdown.

There was a doctrine in the family, which Jane steadfastly supported, if she did not start it, that in all important respects the elder sister was the superior. This view was not many years ago found to persist in a branch of the family, the ladies of which made it plain that Cassandra and her drawing were not less interesting in their eyes than Jane and her writing. Certainly she was a woman of mark in her own circle, much looked up to and deferred to. Neither her sister's tribute to her as 'the finest comic writer of the present age', nor her allusions to her 'starched notions' and her 'dislike of desultory novels', need be taken very seriously. But we may perhaps think of her without injustice as a person of very regular habits and settled opinions.

The fifth son, Francis William (1774–1865), may have got his names from his father's kind uncle Francis Austen and from his grandfather William Austen. Like his youngest brother he was a successful naval officer; but he rose higher and lived longer than Charles, dying at ninety-one, Admiral of the Fleet and G.C.B. Though, from no fault of his own, he missed Trafalgar, he was able to marry, in the following year, Mary Gibson, distinguished in the letters as 'Mrs. F.A.'. She had eleven children

(among them, of course, a Cassandra), and died in
1823. Five years later he married Martha Lloyd,
sister of that Mary Lloyd who was James Austen's
second wife. Martha had long lived with old Mrs.
Austen and her daughters, and acted as honorary
aunt to the Austen nephews and nieces. It is pleasant to know that she lived to be Lady Austen.

The sixth son, Charles John (1779–1852), owed
his names to no obvious source, though there were
Johns among the Kentish Austens; he followed in
Frank's footsteps but at a certain distance, dying at
seventy-two, becoming an admiral but not a knight,
marrying twice but begetting no more than seven
children. As Jane's 'own particular little brother'
he drew out her comic talent for his amusement.[1]

The younger daughter, Jane Austen, who was
born at Steventon 16 December 1775 (four or five
years younger than Wordsworth and Scott) and
died at Winchester, aged forty-one, on 18 July
1817, derived her Christian name, the author of the
Memoir tells us, from her great-grandmother on
her mother's side. It is natural to suppose that the
choice had reference also to her godmother Jane
Austen, the wife of her father's uncle Francis. Her
other godparents were a Mrs. Musgrave, a connexion of her mother, and the Rev. Samuel Cooke,

[1] See p. 161.

who as we saw married Mrs. Austen's cousin. Until five-and-twenty she lived in her father's rectory. Five years were then spent with her parents and sister in Bath, three with her mother and sister and Martha Lloyd in Southampton; in 1809 the party moved to Chawton, and there Jane lived until within a few weeks of her death. The pattern of her life was varied by long visits to London and Kent. If she had a serious love-affair—the history is obscure —it was ended, like her sister's, by death. She had two main periods of literary activity, of which the first belongs to Steventon and to her very early twenties, the second to her last years. But she published nothing until 1811, and all the publications of her lifetime fall within five years. Her death, the cause of which is unknown, followed an illness which lasted rather more than a year.

II

STEVENTON: 1775–1801

GEORGE AUSTEN'S livings of Steventon and Deane in North Hampshire lie within a mile and a half of each other, near the main road from London to Basingstoke, Andover, and Salisbury. Overton, the post-town, is nearly eight miles west of Basingstoke, and Steventon, lying south of the road, is nearly as far from Basingstoke and a mile or two from Overton. Coaches could be caught at Deane Gate on this road, or at Popham Lane, at about the same distance but south of Steventon, on the road from London to Winchester and Southampton.

The country-side is affectionately defined by the author of the *Memoir*, who spent his youth at Steventon, as 'lying in one of the best portions of the Vine Hunt' of which he was the historian. It is not a striking country. Mrs. Austen, who came from Henley, is said to have been disappointed, missing the wide prospects and the noble timber of the Thames valley. The North Hampshire chalk is a thin soil, and does not grow the finest trees. But it is a country of pleasing irregularities, abounding in lanes and lovely farms and cottages, and it is still very little altered for the worse.

The parsonage in which the Austens lived was pulled down more than a hundred years ago. But we know it from sketches by Anna Lefroy and from descriptions. It was little more than a cottage when George Austen entered it, but he added and improved till it was 'sufficiently commodious to hold pupils in addition to a growing family'. The sketches show a front of two stories, with dormered attics above. The 'dining or common sitting-room', which 'looked to the front and was lighted by two casement windows', was perhaps to the right of the front door—the position of the chimneys suggests a kitchen on that side of the house. The front door 'opened into a smaller parlour', where visitors were likely to find Mrs. Austen 'busily engaged with her needle'. The larger room to the left may have been the Rector's study looking to the garden, 'his own exclusive property'; the garden wall is on that side. But the study had a bow-window at the back of the house, and may have been wholly in the added part. On the first floor, we are told, the girls made a dressing-room, 'as they were pleased to call it, perhaps because it opened into a smaller chamber in which my two aunts slept'. Mrs. Lefroy seems to have been unaware of the important and dignified part played by the dressing-room in the economy of the eighteenth century and later. The Steventon

dressing-room must have been of the same size
as the dining-room, with two casements; and the
smaller chamber, presumably, was above the front
door and Mrs. Austen's reception room. Mrs.
Lefroy remembered 'the common-looking carpet
with its chocolate ground, and painted press with
shelves above for books, and Jane's piano'. The
shelves held her copy of Dodsley's *Poems* and the
five volumes of *Camilla*; and this room was the
birthplace of *Pride and Prejudice*. The other large
room on this floor was no doubt the parents'. Where
the boys slept (an object of solicitude to Aunt Jane
elsewhere at a later date)[1] we have to guess. The
three dormers no doubt indicate as many bedrooms,
and more lay behind.

The amount of the Austens' income is not known.
When they left Steventon Mr. Austen hoped to
have not much less than £600 a year, presumably
after provision for two curates.[2] In earlier days he
was rich enough to keep a carriage. It did not suit
him to send his sons to school. Instead he took
pupils in his house, and the boys all learned together.
The writer of a *History of the Leigh Family of Adlestrop*, composed in 1788, gives an unexpected parallel to the lettered simplicity of Steventon. 'With
his sons (all promising to make figures in life)

[1] Letter 90.   Letter 29.

Mr. Austen educates a few youths of chosen friends and acquaintances. When among this liberal society, the simplicity, hospitality and taste which commonly prevail in affluent families among the delightful valleys of Switzerland ever recur to my memory.'[1] Later, two of the elder boys went to Oxford, and one picked up a fortune; the two youngest early found themselves in the King's service.

Probably Mrs. Austen had charge of the little girls' early education. Catherine Morland's sympathetic account of her mother's discharge of this duty—'how stupid they can be for a whole morning together, and how tired my poor mother is at the end of it'—may be reminiscence. But Mrs. Austen was poorer than Mrs. Morland, and therefore busier; and the accommodation of the rectory may well have been strained. So Cassandra and Jane went to school. First, as family tradition records, they and their cousin Jane Cooper were in the charge of a Mrs. Cawley, sister of Dr. Cooper and widow of a Principal of Brasenose; this was at Oxford and later at Southampton, where the sisters caught what was then called a putrid fever. Jane Austen nearly died; and her aunt, Mrs. Cooper, who had carried the girls away, did die. This was in 1783, so Jane must have been very young indeed

[1] *Life* 25.

when her Oxford education began.[1] Next, the sisters went to the Abbey School at Reading.[2] But Jane was only nine when her schooldays ended, and they seem to have made little impression on her. She had been sent to Reading not because she could learn much there, but because Cassandra could not go without her. 'If Cassandra were going to have her head cut off', her mother remarked, 'Jane would insist on sharing her fate.'[3] It has been noticed that none of her heroines were sent to school except Anne Elliot; and the motive there might be convenience, to smooth the introduction of Mrs. Smith.[4]

What Jane may have learned at Steventon, and from whom she learned it, will be best considered when we come to examine her early essays in writing. Whatever she owed to books, she owed more to observation. It is time to look out of the rectory window and see the world on which she sharpened her growing wits.

The Austens had a position above that of what Mrs. Proudie called the inferior parish clergy. George Austen, like Charles Hayter in *Persuasion*, 'had chosen to be a scholar and a gentleman'; his wife was connected with the academic clergy of

---

[1] *Life 25.*   [2] *Life 26.*   [3] *Memoir*, ch. 1.
[4] It was very convenient to send Mary Elliot to school, and so keep her ignorant of Anne's short engagement.

Oxford, and had a pedigree. Moreover, Mr. Austen held a family living where the squire did not reside, and 'shared with the principal tenant the command of an excellent manor'.[1] The Austens naturally enjoyed such society as the neighbourhood afforded. The local magnates deserved a growing satirist's attention. Lord Bolton, who was 'particularly curious in his pigs',[2] was an Orde, a family of whose worldly wisdom Jane thought highly;[3] he married the heiress of the fifth Duke of Bolton, became Orde Powlett, and on the extinction of the dukedom was created Baron Bolton. Lord Dorchester was Guy Carleton, who had been Commander-in-chief in America. Lord Portsmouth, when a small boy, had been one of George Austen's pupils; his eccentricity was early apparent in his 'curiously worded invitations'.[4] But the young Austens' intercourse with such people was probably limited to occasional balls at Hackwood or Kempshott Park or Hurstbourne, or to their presence at Basingstoke assemblies. English society as Jane Austen depicts it shows a sharp cleavage between the nobility and the gentry. The gulf was not impassable; Darcy's mother was an earl's daughter, and General Tilney visited a marquis. But Darcy was a proud man and the

---

[1] *Memoir*, ch. 2.   [2] Letter 13.
[3] Letter 72.   [4] Letter 26.

General an ambitious man. Anne Elliot, a baronet's daughter, 'had never seen her father and sister in contact with nobility'; indeed Miss Elliot had for thirteen years 'been walking immediately after Lady Russell out of all the drawing-rooms and dining-rooms in the country', which means that the Elliots did not dine in noble houses. In the society of East Kent, where Jane was as much at home as in Hampshire, baronets are as thick as blackberries; but there is only a slight infusion of higher rank. I imagine that the reason for this cleavage was in part political. The ruling aristocracy was tradition-ally Whig. The country gentlemen, and their rela-tions the country clergy, were traditionally Tory. In *Sense and Sensibility*[1] the silly Mrs. Palmer explains that her husband in Somerset was not acquainted with Willoughby in Devonshire: 'I do not think Mr. Palmer would visit him, for he is in the opposition you know.' I do not think this kind of feud survived in the Victorian age.

The smaller fry, whom Jane calls 'the meaner and more usual &c. &c.'s', are too numerous to be detailed. But a glance at the map of the road between Whitchurch and Basingstoke will show Freefolk, Laverstock, Ash, Deane, Oakley, and Manydown, where lived Portals, Holders, Har-

[1] i, ch. 20.

woods, Bramstons, and Bigg-Withers. These are names with which the early letters are freely sprinkled. Some of their owners were, no doubt, of the type of the squire who appealed to Mr. Austen to settle a dispute between him and his wife, whether Paris were in France or France in Paris. But there is evidence of superior cultivation. If the conversation sometimes languished, Jane had other resources; 'to sit in idleness over a good fire in a well-proportioned room is a luxurious sensation'.

A few families exact a closer attention. When Jane was thirteen, there came to live in her father's parsonage at Deane a Mrs. Lloyd and her three daughters. Mrs. Lloyd was the widow of a clergyman and the daughter of Governor Craven of South Carolina. Her daughters were Martha, Eliza, and Mary. Eliza, whom readers of the *Letters* must distinguish from Eliza Austen, Henry's wife, had already married her cousin Fulwar Craven Fowle, brother of Cassandra Austen's fiancé. Fowle afterwards succeeded his father as Vicar of Kintbury in Berkshire, and we shall hear of visits to Kintbury. Martha became the close friend of Cassandra and Jane, and lived with them from the Southampton days onwards. Later, as we saw, she became Frank Austen's second wife. Mary married the widowed James Austen in 1797, and was the mother of James

Edward and of Caroline. In 1792 the Lloyds had left Deane and gone to live at Ibthorp,[1] a village near Andover, nearly twenty miles from Steventon. But there were mutual visitings, and we have letters written to and from Ibthorp.

Another friendship was with the family at Manydown. The father and son were Bigg-Wither, but the daughters remained plain Bigg. Three of them concern us: Elizabeth married a Heathcote of Hursley, was early widowed, and was the mother of the Sir William Heathcote who was a figure in the Oxford Movement. Catherine married Herbert Hill, Rector of Streatham and father-in-law of Southey's daughter. Alethea remained unmarried, and lived first with her widowed father, later, in Jane's last years, at Winchester with her widowed sister, Mrs. Heathcote.

The aisle of Steventon Church contains the tombs of several members of the family of Digweed who, in Jane's time and long after, rented the fine Tudor manor-house. One of the Digweeds moved to Alton about the same time that the Austens moved to Chawton; so that in late as well as in early days, Digweeds furnished comic relief to Jane's life and letters.

On a different intellectual plane is the family of

---

[1] J.A. spells it *Ibthrop*; it is pronounced *Ibtrop*.

Mr. Lefroy, Rector of Ashe. His wife was a sister of Sir Egerton Brydges, and the author of the *Memoir* knew her by repute as a very good and very charming woman, whose 'enthusiastic eagerness of disposition rendered her especially attractive to a clever and lively girl'.[1] She was Jane's intimate friend, though twenty-five years her senior. She was killed by a fall from her horse on Jane's birthday, the 16th of December 1804. Four years later, on that day, Jane wrote the lines[2] which are printed in the *Memoir*, 'not for their merits as poetry, but to show how deep and lasting was the impression'. These verses are not poetical, though here and there a line almost achieves poetry. But they show a depth and warmth of feeling of which their writer has often been thought incapable. The same feeling and the same love of goodness are in the novels too, for those who can find them. But they are there concealed by a reticence which is partly native, partly deliberate. Mrs. Lefroy had a nephew who, as we shall see, might have liked to marry Jane, and a son Benjamin who did marry Jane's niece Anna, so that Lefroys are part of the family history to this day.

The portraits of Jane Austen are not satisfactory,[3]

---

[1] *Memoir*, ch. 3.   [2] See p. 143.
[3] See Appendix.

and those who wish to picture her in her youthful bloom must depend on descriptions. Our first witness is her kinswoman Philadelphia Walter, who in 1788 describes her as 'very like her brother Henry, not at all pretty and very prim, unlike a girl of twelve', and as 'whimsical and affected'.[1] Her trouble was, perhaps, precocity and shyness. 'What is become of all the shyness in the world?' she exclaims in later years, contrasting the manners of an agreeable young visitor with 'anything that I was at her age'. Her looks improved, and it is tempting to find autobiography in Catherine Morland's progress from 'very plain' to 'almost pretty'. Egerton Brydges[2] remembered her as his sister's favourite; 'I never suspected that she was an authoress, but my eyes told me that she was fair and handsome, slight and elegant, but with cheeks a little too full.'[3] By 1791, in the opinion of their cousin Eliza —an impulsive witness—both Cassandra and Jane are 'very much grown (the latter is now taller than myself) and greatly improved as well in manners as in person' and are, in short, 'two of the prettiest girls in England'.[4]

The description in the *Memoir*[5] rests on the

<hr>

[1] *Life* 59.
[2] See p. 29.
[3] *Autobiography*, 1834, ii. 41.
[4] *Life* 61.
[5] Ch. 5.

writer's own recollection of his aunt in her late thirties.

In person she was very attractive; her figure was rather tall and slender, her step light and firm, and her whole appearance expressive of health and animation. In complexion she was a clear brunette with a rich colour; she had full round cheeks, with mouth and nose small and well formed, light hazel eyes, and brown hair forming natural curls close round her face. If not so regularly handsome as her sister, yet her countenance[1] had a peculiar charm of its own to the eyes of most beholders.

Henry Austen's portrait is, as we should expect, more ambitious.[2]

Of personal attractions she possessed a considerable share. Her stature was that of true elegance. It could not have been increased without exceeding the middle height. Her carriage and deportment were quiet, yet graceful. Her features were separately good. Their assemblage produced an unrivalled expression of that cheerfulness, sensibility, and benevolence, which were her real characteristics. Her complexion was of the finest texture. It might with truth be said, that her eloquent blood spoke through her modest cheek.[3]

---

[1] *Countenance* is what we now call *expression*. [2] *Biographical Notice*. [3] It may seem surprising to find Donne quoted in such a context in 1818; but I believe *The Second Anniversary* had found its way into a popular anthology. Mr. John Sparrow points out that the lines are quoted in *Spectator* 41 and in *Tom Jones* iv. 2.

This might pass for a portrait of Marianne Dash-wood. It is, I suspect, not very like the portrait which has shaped itself in modern minds. Do not many of us see a lady rather older than her years, seated quietly, perhaps a little stiffly, in a not too well-ventilated drawing-room; her smile friendly, tolerant, but malicious; little subject to impulse, and in no danger of tell-tale motions of the blood?

But this is to anticipate. The young Jane, it would be allowed, shook off any primness, and became animated enough. If she alarmed her elders by the range of her reading and the precocity of her cynicism, she was soon diverting them by the breadth of her comic muse. At the time when the parsonage rafters were vibrating to 'Love and Freindship' and 'unfinished comedies', we have a glimpse of the interior by a gifted visitor. Their cousin Eliza, who after a chequered girlhood had made a brilliant marriage in France, came to stay at Steventon, bringing with her a command of the French language, knowledge of the French court, and a talent for theatricals.[1] 'My uncle's barn' was 'fitted up quite like a theatre, and all the young folk are to take their part'. Philadelphia Walter was

---

[1] *Life*, chapters 3 and 4. She was 'an extremely accomplished woman, not only for that day, but for any day'. Anna Lefroy to J. E. Austen Leigh, April (1869).

urged to join the company, if she were willing to act, for 'my Aunt Austen declares she has not room for any idle young people'. James Austen was employed to write the necessary prologues and epilogues,[1] and possibly to flirt with the leading lady, then a grass widow.[2]

Our knowledge of these performances comes to an end in 1790, when Jane was barely fifteen. It is possible that they may have been resumed after 1794, in Eliza's brief widowhood, at a time when Jane would be more of an age to take part. But even in 1790 she might see all that Fanny Price saw, both of the ostensible and of the hidden drama of rehearsals.

There is no reason to suppose that Jane's life at Steventon was monotonous or her circle narrow. A large and vigorous family party, with much to employ it at home and out of doors, and sufficient if need be for mutual entertainment,[3] but with the added variety of resident pupils and a French countess, might keep a younger daughter busy and amused, even if she had not been a voracious reader

[1] A list of these is in Messrs. Myers & Co.'s catalogue 291 (1933), No. 56. The volume there described contained copies, not James's originals.

[2] See p. 127.

[3] *Life* 51; but we are told that Jane was one of the least exclusive.

and a precocious writer. But in fact there was gaiety
abroad, of which the early letters give a picture;
Cassandra and Jane had congenial friends of their
own age. Jane's faculty of hero-worship found an
object in Mrs. Lefroy, her talent for social satire a
sufficiency of targets. There were visits to Kent, to
Bath, and elsewhere. When the family circle nar-
rowed, there was news: news from Oxford, tragic
news from Paris, stirring news from the high seas.
Brothers married, and Jane early became an aunt.

The few surviving letters which belong to the
last five years at Steventon give a picture of youthful gaiety and of commonplace employments. But
in fact Jane's early twenties had experience of
tragedy, and even of melodrama. Eliza's husband
fell by the guillotine. Another cousin, Jane Williams, was killed in a carriage accident. Cassandra's
love story ended in her lover's death. Finally, in
1799 her uncle's wife, Mrs. Leigh Perrot, was
committed for trial on a charge of petty theft, and
was confined for many months before her acquittal.
It is probable she was the victim of a blackmailer.
It is recorded that Cassandra and Jane volunteered
to join her, but that their aunt rejected the sacrifice
as unsuitable for 'elegant young women'.[1]

[1] *Life*, ch. 9; Sir Frank MacKinnon's *Grand Larceny*, 1937.

III

READING AND WRITING

WHEN Jane Austen was becoming famous she was embarrassed by the attentions of the Regent's librarian, who begged her 'to delineate in some future work the habits of life and character and enthusiasm of a clergyman'.[1] In protesting her incompetence for this task Jane Austen described herself as 'a woman who knows only her mother tongue, and has read little in that. . . . I think I may boast myself to be, with all possible vanity, the most unlearned and uninformed female who ever dared to be an authoress.' When she made this declaration she was guilty—as indeed she confesses—of what Darcy calls the indirect boast; she has been punished by being taken at her own valuation. Those critics whose reading of the novels tells them that the writer's only real interest was in trifles will continue to believe that her self-depreciation was substantially, if not literally, just, and that

It would be difficult to name a writer of similar eminence who possessed so little knowledge of literature.[2]

[1] Letters 113a, 120.
[2] H. W. Garrod in *Essays*, Royal Society of Literature, 1928, p. 29.

But the evidence is against them. Jane was no doubt ignorant of Latin,[1] and probably felt her ignorance painfully when she read Boswell or the *Lives of the Poets*. But she certainly had a working knowledge of French,[2] as with such a cousin as Eliza she could hardly fail to have; and she probably knew as much Italian as Anne Elliot.

Of her English reading we know a good deal.[3] There may be some hyperbole in Henry Austen's statement that 'her reading was very extensive in history and belles lettres, and her memory extremely tenacious', as perhaps there is in his description of his father as 'a profound scholar, possessing a most exquisite taste in every species of literature'. But it is impossible to disbelieve him when he declares, with more precision, that 'it is difficult to say at what age she was not intimately acquainted with the merits and defects of the best essays and novels in the English language'.[4] The *Memoir*,

[1] Yet a casual allusion to 'her sister in Lucina' (Letter 84) shows her not quite innocent of Lemprière.

[2] Note especially Letter 90, where the phrase 'the Bru of feu the Archbishop' shows more than a schoolgirl knowledge.

[3] The title-page of *Love & Freindship*, which is dated June 1790 (when she was fourteen and a half), mentions *The Sorrows of Werter* and shows acquaintance with the sentimental and pica-resque fiction of the century. See Thomson, *Survey*, ch. 2.

[4] The index of literary allusions in volume v (*N.A. and P.*) of my edition of the novels (1923) covered also the minor works and (rather perfunctorily) the letters. Later editions added

equally explicit, tells us that 'every circumstance narrated in Sir Charles Grandison, all that was ever said or done in the cedar parlour, was familiar to her; and the wedding days of Lady L. and Lady G. were as well remembered as if they had been living friends'.

She refers several times to books in her own possession. These have long been known to include Goldsmith's *History of England*, with her youthful marginalia, and Dodsley's *Collection of Poems*, and Fanny Burney's *Camilla*, for which she was a subscriber in 1796. A more recent accidental dispersal revealed her ownership of Hume's *History*, Thomson's *Works*, Goldsmith's *Animated Nature*, Hayley's *Poems and Plays*. These volumes contain her signature, and the dates of acquisition, always before 1800. Some of them have also the bookplate of her uncle, James Leigh Perrot, who must have given them to her. Her possession of such books gives us a light on the attitude of her elders to her precocious ambitions.

When the family left Steventon the furniture was sold. Carriage was costly, and their way of living

some references which I had overlooked and included *Sanditon* (first published 1925). This list was superseded, for the letters, by the index of authors, books, and plays, appended to my edition of the *Letters* (1932).

in Bath uncertain. The sacrifice of Jane's modest library, and of her father's five hundred volumes, must have been a necessary sacrifice, which the prospect of good circulating libraries would lighten.[1] But the books were not dispersed. It is clear from the letters, and from their later history, that they, like the furniture, were 'bought in' by James Austen at the sale, and his son inherited them. Some of them have his signature or bookplate.[2]

The literary allusions in the novels are not numerous, nor very significant. The letters are more informative. Most of the references are to novels; but these are not always contemporary novels from the library. Jane had read *Tom Jones* before she was twenty, and she mentions *Tristram Shandy* and *A Sentimental Journey*. Smollett is not mentioned. She knew both *The Female Quixote* and *The Spiritual Quixote*, and was of course familiar with Madame D'Arblay and Miss Edgeworth. She was an early victim to the fascination of Mrs. Radcliffe and her school; the horrid novels named by

[1] A scrap of later acquisition has survived. This is a copy of Richard Warner's *Excursion from Bath*, 1801, inscribed on the title-page: 'Geo: Austen 4 Sydney Terrace 1802' and on a fly-leaf: 'J. Austen Southampton 1807'. On p. 332, at a mention of a woollen works 'called New-Mill belongs to Messrs. Austin', is a note (I believe) in J. A.'s hand: 'A haunt of the Austens—"the Gray Coats of Kent".'

[2] *Book Collector's Quarterly*, July–Sept. 1933, 28.

Isabella Thorpe are real books, and Jane had read
them all.

Outside the novel her reading, though not recon-
dite, was sufficiently wide. She often mentions
Shakespeare, and Henry Crawford knew that
'Shakespeare one gets acquainted with without
knowing how. It is a part of an Englishman's
constitution.' Milton is just mentioned, but in a
way that may show knowledge.[1] For the rest, her
poets are the obvious poets—Pope, Thomson,
Gray, Cowper, Crabbe, Scott, Byron. There is no
mention of Burns or of Wordsworth except in
Sanditon. In prose she is more discursive. Though
she confesses distaste for fat quartos, she did not
quail before Henry's *History of England* which, like
Hume's, is in six volumes quarto. She knew Johnson as well as Boswell, and Baretti's travel books,
and Blair's *Rhetoric*, and Sherlock's *Sermons*. 'At a
very early age she was enamoured of Gilpin on the
Picturesque', and was no doubt acquainted with
Price, and Payne Knight, and other polemical
writers on landscape and landscape-gardening.

She is thinking of her own education when she
makes Elizabeth Bennet defend the want of a

[1] 'Your Aunt C. quite enters into the exquisiteness of that
name. Newton Priors is really a Nonpareil. Milton would have
given his eyes to have thought of it', Letter 100.

governess at Longbourn. 'Such of us as wished to learn, never wanted the means. We were always encouraged to read, and had all the masters that were necessary.' Perhaps no masters came to Steventon from Basingstoke; but with such parents and brothers, Jane hardly wanted them. That a bookish family atmosphere was familiar to her is plain from the novels, and especially from *Mansfield Park*, which is more bookish than its plot at all requires.[1] Marianne Dashwood's 'favourite topics for discourse' were almost all literary and artistic—the beauties of Cowper and Scott, the limitations of Pope, second marriages, and picturesque beauty.[2] Catherine Morland, though her ignorance was almost as captivating as her beauty, had learned from books the spell of romance; 'her passion for ancient edifices was next in degree to her passion for Henry Tilney—and castles and abbies made usually the charm of those reveries which his image did not fill.' Even Elizabeth, who of all the heroines had the greatest social talent and the greatest temptation to exercise it on men rather than on books, had taught herself to read, and was ready to talk about books. She was not only transported by the pros-

---

[1] We should hardly have supposed, if we had not been told so, that Tom Bertram and his sisters read aloud well.

[2] *Sense and Sensibility*, i. 10.

pect of a picturesque tour—'adieu to disappointment and spleen; what are men to rocks and moun-
tains?'—but resolved to write an account of her
travels.[1]

The author of the *Memoir* was unable to say how
early his aunt began to write, but knew that her
childish tales 'had amounted to a considerable number by the time she was sixteen'. Three volumes
of her 'effusions' have survived, of which two have
been published.[2] The dates suggest that these
belong to the age between fifteen and eighteen.
The volumes contain a large number of pieces,
narrative or dramatic, for the most part very short,
which we may suppose intended to be read or
enacted in the family circle. They would lend
themselves to costume and to gag. Even without
such aid, and at this distance of time, some of them
are very entertaining and can hardly be read aloud
with gravity.

The juvenile pieces are almost all farcical. One
of them, *Catherine* (or *Kitty*) *and the Bower*, which
is still unpublished, is interesting as a very early
essay in serious fiction. An extract from it, given
in the *Life*,[3] shows that the writer was taking a
subject suggested by her family history.

---

[1] *Pride and Prejudice*, ii. 4.   [2] See p. 161.
[3] p. 31. (See on Philadelphia Austen, p. 13 above.)

Our knowledge of the composition of the early
novels starts from a note made by Cassandra and
quoted in the *Life*[1] as follows:

> *First Impressions* (original of *Pride and Prejudice*),
>   begun October 1796, ended August 1797.
> *Sense and Sensibility*, begun November 1797.
> *Northanger Abbey*, written in 1797 and 1798.

But the *Memoir*[2] knew of an earlier form of *Sense
and Sensibility*, called *Elinor and Marianne*, which
was earlier than *First Impressions*. Caroline Austen
wrote (1869), 'Memory is treacherous, but I cannot
be mistaken in saying that Sense and Sensibility was
first written in letters, and *so* read to her family.'
We cannot hope to know anything about *Elinor and
Marianne*, which must have been completely recast.
As the authors of the *Life* point out, it is difficult to
guess between whom the letters passed, since in the
book as we know it the sisters are never apart.

First Impressions, then, may be regarded as Jane
Austen's first completed novel. There are two references to it in the early letters.[3] In January 1799 she
writes to Cassandra, 'I do not wonder at your want-
ing to read "First Impressions" again, so seldom as
you have gone through it, and that so long ago.' In
June she writes: 'I would not let Martha read "First
Impressions" again upon any account, and am very

[1] p. 96.   [2] p. 49.   [3] Letters 17, 21.

glad that I did not leave it in your power. She is very cunning, but I saw through her design; she means to publish it from memory, and one more perusal must enable her to do it.'

First Impressions, when it was finished, must have been read and approved by the author's father; for on 1 November 1797 he wrote the following letter[1] to Cadell the publisher:

Sir—I have in my possession a manuscript novel, comprising 3 vols., about the length of Miss Burney's Evelina. As I am well aware of what consequence it is that a work of this sort should make its first appearance under a respectable name, I apply to you. I shall be much obliged therefore if you will inform me whether you choose to be concerned in it, what will be the expense of publishing it at the author's risk, and what you will venture to advance for the property of it, if on perusal it is approved of. Should you give any encouragement, I will send you the work.

　　　　　I am, Sir, your humble servant,
　　　　　　　　　　George Austen.

This was not a very businesslike inquiry, for the alternatives—that the publisher should be paid or should pay—are not clearly stated as such. No encouragement was given, and the project dropped.

A second attempt was at first more successful. In

---

[1] We owe our knowledge of this letter to a member of the Lefroy family, who bought it at Cadell's sale.

the spring of 1803 'a MS novel in two vols., entitled *Susan*' was sold for £10 to the publisher Crosby with a view to immediate publication. This transaction was effected by a Mr. Seymour, who must have been Henry Austen's man of business of that name. Crosby duly advertised 'Susan; a Novel in 2 Volumes'; but went no farther. The book, as we shall find, was *Northanger Abbey*.

It is generally said that Jane Austen had two periods of literary activity—her early twenties and her late thirties—and that these were separated by a long interval of inactivity. We have no certain evidence of composition in the period between Steventon and Chawton, except her own statement that *Northanger Abbey* was 'finished' in 1803. It is likely, on the other hand, that revision and experiment went on. But the letters have no references to writing. It is certain that there was in this period no such fertility as that which, earlier and later, produced six novels in about as many years.

Various reasons have been suggested for this failure of an early inspiration. There is no positive evidence, and we cannot forbear to guess. Perhaps the fiasco of *Susan*—more cruelly disappointing than an immediate rebuff—is a sufficient explanation. No one, I suppose, can long endure the labour of writing novels with no expectation of seeing them in print; and Jane Austen seems to have made up her mind that the publishers did not want her. For when at last she decided to publish, she did so at her own expense. The straitened circumstances which followed her father's death may have made publication in those times impossible, or morally impossible. The Chawton benefaction, perhaps, made just the difference.

Something, moreover, may be due to the uncongenial way of life—unsettled and unsettling—in lodgings or temporary houses in Bath and Southampton. Finally, we have to estimate as best we may the shock of emotional experiences of which the scanty evidences are discussed in Chapter V.

IV

BATH AND SOUTHAMPTON: 1801-9

THERE were many good reasons for the decision to leave Steventon. Mr. Austen was now seventy, and might with a good conscience resign his duties[1] to his son and destined successor. Mrs. Austen's health was uncertain. The family circle was sadly shrunken; and Cassandra, since her bereavement, had spent much of her time with her brother at Godmersham.

The tradition is that when, in November 1800, Jane returned from a visit to Ibthorp and was told that it was 'all settled', she fainted.[2] Our best authority is Caroline Austen, who wrote to her brother:[3]

My Aunt was very sorry to leave her native home, as I have heard my Mother relate. My Aunts[4] had been away a little while, and were met in the Hall on their return by their Mother who told them it was all settled, and they were going to live at Bath. My Mother who was present said my Aunt was greatly distressed. All things were done in a hurry by Mr. Austen.

---

[1] It would not then be expected that he should resign the living.   [2] *Life* 155.

[3] 1 April (1869).

[4] Jane and Martha—not Cassandra, who was at Godmersham.

Jane made the best of it. We may guess that she thought a change of scene would be good for Cassandra, who could not always be in Kent.

I get more and more reconciled to the idea of our removal. We have lived long enough in this neighbourhood, the Basingstoke Balls are certainly on the decline, there is something interesting in the bustle of going away, and the prospect of spending future summers by the Sea or in Wales is very delightful.[1]

But it has been noted[2] as significant that there are no letters to Cassandra between the time of the decision and the following January. Letters must have been written, for Cassandra was at Godmersham. That they were destroyed suggests that they were not of the ordinary cheerful kind. Jane's local attachments were of extraordinary strength; they were no small part of her genius. We cannot doubt that the loss of her native county, and of the multitude of associations which made up her girlish experience, was exquisitely painful. Her feelings cannot have been less acute than Marianne's on leaving Norland, or Anne's on leaving Kellynch. Her return to her own country, eight years later, was the long-delayed return of an exile. It is clear, moreover, that she disliked towns in themselves, for their confinement and their meaningless bustle. She reveals

---

[1] Letter 29.   [2] *Life* 156.

herself in Anne Elliot, who 'persisted in a very determined, though very silent, disinclination for Bath', resigning herself to a long 'imprisonment' there,[1] and in poor Fanny's endurance of the glare and squalor of Portsmouth.

The years spent in Bath were clouded by Cassandra's tragedy and (in a degree which can only be conjectured) by Jane's own frustration and her blunder at Manydown.[2] Even if the sisters had not had those sorrows, their life in Sydney Terrace and Green Park Buildings might have been drab enough. Their father's powers were failing, and their mother was for some time seriously ill. Their only relations were the Leigh Perrots in Paragon. Jane was fond of her uncle, but did not pretend to like his wife. They had many casual acquaintances, but made no friends. In earlier visits Jane had enjoyed the parade of Bath with no less than Catherine Morland's gusto. Her aunt's large parties were less amusing now, and perhaps she might have said, with Anne, that she had 'no pleasure in this sort of meeting'.[3]

We have very few letters of these years, in which the sisters were seldom apart. Conjecture is hazardous, but it is a reasonable conjecture that Jane's natural cheerfulness was severely tried, and that the annual 'ramble', to which she had looked for com-

---

[1] *Persuasion* ii. 2, 3.   [2] See p. 61.   [3] *Persuasion* ii. 10.

pensation, was in fact her chief source of pleasure. The family party seems to have spent part of each year on the coast of Dorset or South Devon; and it is almost certain that Jane was at Lyme Regis in November 1803—the month in which it was later visited by the Musgroves.

The chronology of her writings cannot be determined. It is impossible to say that in any year she was not doing something, at least in the way of revision. But it is certain that she did not recapture, either in Bath or in Southampton, the creative impulse of the last years at Steventon. She did not, however, entirely give up writing in Bath. We know from herself that *Northanger Abbey* was 'finished in 1803'; the short sketch entitled *Lady Susan* and the ten chapters of the unfinished *Watsons* may belong to this period.

The manuscripts of *The Watsons* and of *Lady Susan* are written on paper with watermarks dated 1803 and 1805 respectively. There is a fair presumption that an original manuscript was composed not long after the date of the paper. At a time when paper was costly,[1] it was unlikely that any considerable quantity of it would remain unused in a family

---

[1] Catherine Morland could not exercise her talent for drawing unless she 'could obtain the outside of a letter, or seize upon any other odd piece of paper'.

given to writing. *The Watsons* may therefore with some confidence be assigned to this period. But the manuscript of *Lady Susan*, being a fair copy, really proves no more than that at some time in, or not long after, 1805 Jane Austen was still sufficiently interested in the piece to be at the trouble of making a copy of it.

So promising a story as *The Watsons* has naturally been the subject of speculation—how it would have been continued, why it was abandoned. Several 'continuations' have been published, of which one deserves notice, since it claims to be authoritative. 'The Watsons by Jane Austen, completed in accordance with her intentions by Edith (her great grand-niece) and Francis Brown' was published in 1928. Mrs. Brown tells us that 'Cassandra used to read *The Watsons* aloud to her nieces, and my grandmother, Mrs. Hubback, was one of them . . . she was a favourite with Cassandra'. In 1850 Mrs. Hubback published a novel in three volumes, *The Younger Sister*, which her granddaughter describes as 'Jane Austen through a haze of memory'. The work of 1928 is an attempt 'to disentangle Jane's story from that of her niece'. But the assumption that Mrs. Hubback knew the original author's intentions seems to be slenderly based.

It is usually idle to conjecture the motives which

cause authors to leave work unfinished. The *Memoir*[1]
suggests that Jane Austen became aware 'of the evil
of having placed her heroine too low, in a position
of poverty and obscurity'. This is not a convincing
theory. She is unlikely to have embarked upon the
story without seeing where it would lead her; and
she was neither ignorant of the life of the lower
middle class, nor afraid of vulgarity. Mrs. Brown[2]
thinks the motive was one of delicacy; Emma Watson's situation, in living with a brother and his wife,
was too like Jane's at Southampton. But there is no
real parallel. Emma Watson was to live with her
brother as a dependant; Frank Austen merely joined
forces with his mother and sister, with no loss of
independence on either side.

I have no wish to add to these conjectures. But
The Watsons may with some plausibility be regarded
as a sketch for *Emma*. The scene of both is Surrey.
Mr. Watson is a faint adumbration of Mr. Woodhouse. Mrs. Robert Watson is strikingly sug-
gestive of Mrs. Elton. Emma Watson is very like
Jane Fairfax in situation, and—so far as we get
to know her—not unlike Emma Woodhouse in
character.

Lady Susan is generally thought to be an early

---

[1] 1871; prefatory note to *The Watsons*.
[2] *The Watsons completed*, p. 7.

work. There is no evidence that the author gave it that title, and the fact that she intended to publish *Susan* in 1803 does not prove the abandonment of an intention to publish the shorter piece. But *Lady Susan* can hardly have been designed for separate publication, if any publication was contemplated.[1]

Mary Augusta Austen Leigh[2] was confident that *Lady Susan* was a portrait of the grandmother of the Lloyd girls—Mrs. Lloyd's mother Mrs. Craven, a beautiful woman of fashion who treated her daughters with cruel negligence. The general question of Jane Austen's use of real people and real incidents is discussed later.[3] *Lady Susan* may have had a literary origin. The story is in a manner which the author did not repeat, but which she here handles very unlike a novice. It is as brilliant as its central figure. Its manner is no doubt superior to its matter. The tale is not, as a tale, too convincing, and the characters are not very well individualized. But the hard polish of the style creates a vivid illusion. I hope I am not being fanciful when I find it reminding me of Henry James's early manner: of *Roderick Hudson* and *The Tragic Muse*.

Mr. Austen's death early in 1805 was followed

---

[1] It would not make 200 pages, even in the lavish style in which the novels were first printed.

[2] See p. 169.   [3] See p. 127.

by eighteen months of discomfort and uncertainty. While he lived, they had been comfortably off in a house of their own,[1] and able sometimes to leave Bath. His death left his widow with a very small income. But her sons made it up to a more adequate amount;[2] it was soon settled that Martha Lloyd should make her home with them; and ultimately a further alliance was made with Frank and his young wife in Southampton.[3] Meanwhile they had to be content with lodgings in Bath. Cassandra and Jane were able to visit Kent in the summer of 1805. But it was not until July 1806 that they finally left Bath —'with what happy feelings of escape'[4]—for Clifton. They soon moved again, to visit Mrs. Austen's relations at Adlestrop and at Stoneleigh, where Jane found herself, perhaps for the first time, an inmate of one of the great historic houses of England.[5] She might now fancy herself at Pemberley.

The party moved into lodgings at Southampton in the autumn, and before long were settled in a good house in Castle Square, with a good garden, where Jane was able to indulge her taste. The

[1] With a man and two maids.
[2] £460. *Life* 182.
[3] *Life* 197.
[4] Letter 54.
[5] An amusing account of the visit by Mrs. Austen is quoted in *Life* 196, and at greater length by Miss Hill, ch. 15.

gardener, she writes, 'at my own particular desire procures us some syringas. I could not do without a syringa, for the sake of Cowper's line. We talk also of a laburnum.' Southampton was a pleasant town then. Miss Mitford, who visited it in 1812, called it 'all life, all gaiety', noting 'the total absence of the vulgar hurry of business or the chilling apathy of fashion'.[1] We have a good many letters of the Southampton years, thanks to Cassandra's annual visit to Godmersham, and they are cheerful and lively. Frank's wife was congenial, and Martha was always a comfort. But the society of the place offered few attractions, and there is nothing to suggest that it supplied Jane with any theme or any incentive to write.

In October 1808 Edward Austen lost his wife, who died, very suddenly, soon after the birth of a child. Cassandra was with him at the time. Jane and her mother looked after his two boys, then at Winchester. His loss may have made him feel that he ought to do more for his mother and sisters; and the offer of a house, near Godmersham or at Chawton, was made immediately. Mrs. Austen's choice was for Chawton. This would not mean greater proximity, for Chawton House was let; but Edward no doubt visited his Hampshire estates from time

---

[1] Quoted by Miss Hill, ch. 14.

to time,[1] and may have already foreseen that in years to come he would spend more of his time there.

The offer was accepted with grateful alacrity. Frank and his wife must be left; but Chawton Cottage had room for Martha. In April 1809 the three Austens left Southampton for Godmersham, and in July they were in their new home. Our first letter[2] from Chawton was written to congratulate Frank on the birth of a son. Jane's feelings were too much for her—she breaks into rhyme.

> Cassandra's pen will paint our state,
> The many comforts that await
> Our Chawton home, how much we find
> Already in it, to our mind;
> And how convinced, that when complete
> It will all other Houses beat
> That ever have been made or mended
> With rooms concise, or rooms distended.

She had made up her mind to be happy, and perhaps had already determined on her great adventure.

[1] Letter 60 contemplates the accommodation of his manservant at the cottage.
[2] 68.

V

ROMANCE

WHEN James Austen became engaged to
Mary Lloyd, Mrs. Austen wrote her a letter
of congratulation and welcome, which has been preserved.[1] 'I look forward to you as a real comfort in
my old age when Cassandra is gone into Shropshire and Jane—the Lord knows where.'

That both sisters would marry seemed a matter
of course. Cassandra was already engaged to Thomas
Fowle,[2] for whom his kinsman and friend Lord
Craven intended the living of Ryton in Shropshire.
He went with Lord Craven to the West Indies as
chaplain, and there died of yellow fever in February
1797. Eliza de Feuillide wrote: 'Jane says that her
sister behaves with a degree of resolution and propriety, which no common mind could evince in so
trying a situation.' We hear of no second attachment—'the only thoroughly natural, happy, and
sufficient cure'.[3]

Of Jane's own love-affairs the details are obscure

[1] *Life* 74.
[2] His younger brother Fulwar Craven Fowle had married
Eliza Lloyd, sister of Martha and Mary.
[3] *Persuasion* i. 4.

and the importance uncertain. The first aspirant of whom we hear is Tom Lefroy, nephew of the Rector of Ashe, where he was staying when Jane was twenty. Her own language suggests a very mild flirtation.

At length the day is come on which I am to flirt my last with Tom Lefroy, and when you receive this it will be over. My tears flow at the melancholy idea.[1]

Lefroy became Chief Justice of Ireland, and lived to 1869. The letters in which Jane mentions him were not known to the author of the *Memoir*; but the story had not been forgotten. His sister Caroline writes of it with some heat.[2]

I think I need not warn *you* against raking up that old story of the still living Chief Justice. That there was something in it, is true—but nothing out of the common way (as *I* believe). Nothing to call ill usage, and no very serious sorrow endured. The *York* Lefroys got up a very strong version of it all, and spread their own notions in the family—but they were for years very angry with their kinsman, and rather delighted in a proof as *they* thought, of his early heartlessness. I have *my* story from my Mother, who was near at the time. It was a disappointment, but Mrs. Lefroy sent the gentleman off at the end of a *very* few weeks, that no more mischief might be done. If *his* love had continued a few more years, he *might* have sought her out again—

---

[1] Letter 2 (Jan. 1796).　　　　　　[2] 1 April (1869).

as he was *then* making enough to marry on—but who
can wonder that he did *not*? He was settled in Ireland,
and he married an Irish lady, who certainly *had* the convenience of *money*—there was *no* engagement, and never
had been.

J. E. Austen Leigh applied also to T. E. Lefroy,
the Chief Justice's nephew, who replied:[1]

You have already given in a few sentences the chief
part of what my late venerable uncle told me. He did
not state in what her fascination consisted, but he said in
so many words that he was in love with her, although
he qualified his confession by saying it was a boyish love.
As this occurred in a friendly and private conversation,
I feel some doubt whether I ought to make it public.

The author of the *Memoir* took the advice he was
given, limiting himself to the cautious statement
that 'these two bright young persons were, for a
short time, intimately acquainted'.

The parting with Tom Lefroy may have meant
rather more to Jane than she admitted at the time.
Three years later[2] she reports a visit from Mrs.
Lefroy

with whom, in spite of interruptions . . . , I was enough
alone to hear all that was interesting, which you will
easily credit when I tell you that of her nephew she said
nothing at all, and of her friend very little. She did not
once mention the name of the former to *me*, and I was

[1] 16 Aug. 1870.   [2] Letter 11 (Nov. 1798).

too proud to make any enquiries; but on my father's afterwards asking where he was, I learnt that he was gone back to London in his way to Ireland, where he is called to the Bar and means to practise.

But who was Mrs. Lefroy's 'friend'? He is not named in the letter, but it gives a clue to his identity as well as some account of his interest in the writer.

She showed me a letter which she had received from her friend a few weeks ago (in answer to one written by her to recommend a nephew of Mrs. Russell to his notice at Cambridge), towards the end of which was a sentence to this effect: 'I am very sorry to hear of Mrs. Austen's illness. It would give me particular pleasure to have an opportunity of improving my acquaintance with that family—with a hope of creating to myself a nearer interest. But at present I cannot indulge any expectation of it'. This is rational enough; there is less love and more sense in it than sometimes appeared before, and I am very well satisfied. It will all go on exceedingly well, and decline away in a very reasonable manner. There seems no likelihood of his coming into Hampshire this Christmas, and it is therefore most probable that our indifference will soon be mutual, unless his regard, which appeared to spring from knowing nothing of me at first, is best supported by never seeing me.

If Jane was as indifferent as she says, the identity of her admirer is of no great consequence. He has,

however, been probably identified.[1] Mrs. Russell
was presumably a relative of a Dr. Russell who had
preceded Mr. Lefroy as Rector of Ashe. The friend,
to whom Mrs. Lefroy recommended Mrs. Russell's
nephew, was clearly a Cambridge don. Very few
Cambridge dons figure in the Austen circle; but we
know from a letter written years later that Jane had
been acquainted with Mr. Blackall of Emmanuel.
Writing to her brother Frank in 1813[2] she mentions having noticed Mr. Blackall's 'succeeding to a
College Living, the very Living which we remembered his talking of and wishing for'—she names
the living, which was an Emmanuel living—and
having learned, a few months later, of his marriage
to a Miss Lewis.

I should very much like to know what sort of a Woman
she is. He was a piece of Perfection, noisy Perfection
himself whom I always recollect with regard. . . . I
would wish Miss Lewis to be of a silent turn and rather
ignorant, but naturally intelligent and wishing to learn;
—fond of cold veal pies, green tea in the afternoon, and
a green window blind at night.

There was a family tradition of an affair between
Jane and a Mr. Blackall, though we shall find that
it seems to have been confused with a quite different
episode.

[1] By the authors of the *Life*, p. 86.   [2] Letter 81.

The *Memoir*[1] states guardedly that 'In her youth
she had declined the addresses of a gentleman who
had the recommendations of a good character, and
connections, and position in life, of everything, in
fact, except the subtle power of touching her heart.'
This episode is told with much greater fullness,
though still without names, in the *Life*.[2] It is there
told on the authority of Caroline Austen, whose
mother must have known exactly what happened.
In November 1802 Cassandra and Jane went back
to Steventon to stay with their brother. While
there they paid a visit to their old friends at Manydown. The owner of Manydown was Mr. Bigg-
Wither, a widower. His son Harris was then
twenty-one. His daughters Catherine and Alethea
Bigg[3] were still unmarried, and their sister Elizabeth Heathcote was recently widowed. On Friday
3 December the sisters reappeared at Steventon,
unexpected and in agitation, and insisted, with no
explanation, on James's driving them back to Bath
the next day. The explanation given later was that
Harris Bigg-Wither had proposed to Jane, and that
she had accepted him, only to change her mind next
morning.[4]

[1] Ch. 2.   [2] p. 92.
[3] *not* Wither.
[4] See Chronology, p. 177, for unpublished dates.

The anonymity of the story[1] is explained by letters written to Austen Leigh when he was compiling the *Memoir*. Caroline Austen wrote: 'My own wish would be that not any allusion should be made to the Manydown story, or at *least* that the reference should be so vague, as to give *no* clue to the place or person.' Mr. Wither's children (he had consoled himself in 1804) were still living in the neighbourhood, and the story, though 'as good as dead', would be easily revived.

Another letter[2] is from one of Frank's daughters, Catherine Hubback. She was not born when her Aunt Jane died, but in later years saw a great deal of her Aunt Cassandra.

I gathered from the letters[3] that it was in a momentary fit of self-delusion that Aunt Jane accepted Mr. Wither's proposal, and that when it was all settled eventually, and the negative decisively given she was much relieved. I think the affair vexed her a good deal, but I am sure she had no attachment to him.

The few references to 'Harris' in the extant letters are quite colourless, but mention ill health.[4] If, as

[1] The name was first given by Miss Hill.

[2] 1 March 1870.

[3] This seems to show that Cassandra had allowed her niece to read some of the intimate letters which she later destroyed. See p. 142.

[4] Letters 17, 18, 23, 25 (p. 85).

seems probable, the affair happened soon after Jane's
one serious love-affair, it is natural to suppose that
her mind had lost its normal balance.

What has been called the 'nameless and dateless'
romance is the most elusive of them all. The evidence is so full of obscurities and contradictions
that it cannot fairly be summarized, but must
be presented in full. We must begin with the
Memoir.[1]

There is one passage of romance in her history with
which I am imperfectly acquainted, and to which I am
unable to assign name, or date, or place, though I have
it on sufficient authority. Many years after her death,
some circumstances induced her sister Cassandra to
break through her habitual reticence, and to speak of it.
She said that, while staying at some seaside place, they
became acquainted with a gentleman, whose charm of
person, mind and manners was such that Cassandra
thought him worthy to possess and likely to win her
sister's love. When they parted, he expressed his intention of soon seeing them again; and Cassandra felt
no doubt as to his motives. But they never again met.
Within a short time they heard of his sudden death. I
believe that, if Jane ever loved, it was this unnamed
gentleman; but the acquaintance had been short, and I
am unable to say whether her feelings were of such a
nature as to affect her happiness.

The evidence on which the author of the *Memoir*

[1] Ch. 2.

founded this careful statement has been preserved. One of his main helpers was his half-sister Anna Lefroy. Her daughter, Mrs. Bellas, wrote down the following story.

The Austens with their two daughters were once at Teignmouth, the date of that visit was not later than 1802, but besides this they were once travelling in Devonshire, moving about from place to place, and I think that tour was before they left Steventon in 1801, perhaps as early as 1798 or 1799.[1]

It was while they were so travelling, according to Aunt Cassandra's account many years afterwards, that they somehow made acquaintance with a gentleman of the name of Blackall. He and Aunt Jane mutually attracted each other, and such was his charm that even Aunt Cassandra thought him worthy of her sister. They parted on the understanding that he was to come to Steventon, but instead came I know not how long after a letter from his brother to say that he was dead. There is no record of Jane's affliction, but I think this attachment must have been very deep. Aunt Cassandra herself had so warm a regard for him that some years after her sister's death, she took a good deal of trouble to find out and see again his brother.

Extract of a letter from our dear Aunt Caroline to Mary Leigh.

I have no doubt that Aunt Jane was beloved of several

---

[1] See Chronology. 1802 seems to be the date of the Teignmouth visit, 1801 that of the Sidmouth visit. An earlier seaside tour does not seem very probable.

in the course of her life and was herself very capable of
loving. I wish I could give you more dates as to Mr.
Blackall. All that I know is this. At Newtown Aunt
Cassandra was staying with us[1] when we made the
acquaintance of a certain Mr. Henry Eldridge of the
Engineers. He was very pleasing and very good looking. My Aunt was much struck with him, and *I* was
struck by her commendation as she rarely admired anyone. Afterwards she spoke of him as one so unusually
gifted with all that was agreeable, and said he had
reminded her strongly of a gentleman whom they had
met one Summer when they were by the sea (I think she
said in Devonshire) who had seemed greatly attracted
by my Aunt Jane. That when they parted (I imagine he
was a visitor there also, but his family might have lived
near) he was urgent to know where they would be the
next summer, implying or perhaps saying that he should
be there also wherever it might be. I can only say the
impression left on Aunt Cassandra's mind was that he
had fallen in love with Aunt Jane. Soon afterwards they
heard of his death. I am sure she thought him worthy of
her sister from the way she recalled his memory, and
also that she did not doubt either that he would have
been a successful suitor. Frog Firle 1870.[2]

An inconsistency in the story may be noted at
once. Mrs. Bellas's statement that the suitor was

[1] Caroline and her mother.
[2] Part of this document corresponds closely, though not
exactly, with Caroline Austen's written statement (1870)
quoted in *Life* 89–90.

expected at Steventon does not tally with the corresponding part of her quotation from Caroline's letter.

We have a second account by Caroline in a letter[1] written to her brother at the time of the compilation of the *Memoir*.

During the few years my grandfather lived at Bath, he went in the summer with his wife and daughters to *some* sea-side. They were in Devonshire, and in Wales[2]— and in Devonshire an acquaintance was made with some very charming man—I never heard Aunt Cassandra speak of anyone else with such admiration—she had no doubt that a mutual attachment was in progress between him and her sister. They parted—but he made it plain that he should seek them out again—and shortly afterwards he died. My Aunt told me this in the late years of her own life, and it was quite new to me then—but all this, being nameless and dateless, cannot I know serve any purpose of yours—and it brings no contradiction to your theory that Aunt Jane never *had* any attachment that overclouded her happiness, for long. *This* had not gone far enough to leave misery behind.

Nameless and dateless contradicts the mention of Mr. Blackall in the other letter.

A somewhat different account is given by Mrs.

---

[1] Not dated.

[2] Letter 29 (Jan. 1801) speaks of Wales, in general terms, as a possible alternative to 'summers by the sea'. We have other evidence of a Welsh visit.

Hubback (Francis Austen's daughter Catherine) in letters of 1 and 14 March 1870:

If ever she *was* in love it was with Dr. Blackall (I think that was the name) whom they met at some watering-place, shortly before they settled at Chawton. There is no doubt she admired him extremely, and perhaps regretted parting, but she always said her books were her children, and supplied her sufficient interest for happiness; and some of her letters, triumphing over the married women of her acquaintance, and rejoicing in her own freedom from care were most amusing.

I do not think Dr. Blackall died until long afterwards. If I do not mistake there were two brothers, one of whom was called Mr. Edward B- and I never heard what became of him. The other, the Dr., Aunt Cassandra met with again long afterwards when she made an excursion to the Wye in company with Uncle Charles, two of his daughters and my sister Cassandra. My cousin Cassie Austen, the only survivor of that party, could I have no doubt tell when and how they met him— I only remember that my Aunt found him stout, red-faced and middle-aged—very different from their youthful hero. It must have been in '32 or thereabouts, and I believe he died soon afterwards.

Finally we have a note by Mrs. Bellas in her copy of the Brabourne Letters.[1]

In the summer of 1801 the father, mother and daughters made a tour in Devonshire. They went to Teignmouth,

---

[1] First printed by Miss Thomson, *Survey*, p. 202.

Starcross, Sidmouth etc. I believe it was at the last named place that they made acquaintance with a young clergyman when visiting his brother, who was one of the doctors of the town. He and Jane fell in love with each other, and when the Austens left he asked to be allowed to join them again further on in their tour, and the permission was given. But instead of his arriving as expected, they received a letter announcing his death. In Aunt Cassandra's memory he lived as one of the most charming persons she had known, worthy even in her eyes of Aunt Jane.

The story, as it circulated in the second and third generations, was seriously confused by mistakes and conjectures.[1] Yet I think it must be accepted as substantially true. Cassandra and Caroline were women of accurate minds and long memories. It is difficult to suppose that Cassandra could have been in error about a story so like her own tragic story, or could have given her niece a false impression of it. We may believe, then, with Cassandra, that it would have been a love-match on both sides, and that its frustration was by death.

How deep a mark it made on Jane's life can only

[1] The name *Blackall* is probably a mere error. The Sidmouth directories give the names of several medical men, but no Blackall. The Blackalls were a West Country family, which made the confusion natural. If the story is true in essentials, its hero could not be Samuel Blackall, who as we have seen lived and prospered.

be guessed. The *Memoir*[1] quotes the suggestion of the Quarterly Reviewer,[2] that Fanny Price's love-story was the work of 'a female writing from recollection', only to reject it. 'This conjecture, however probable, was wide of the mark. The picture was drawn from the intuitive perceptions of genius, not from personal experience.' Certainly the Sidmouth story as we have it is very unlike poor Fanny Price's long-drawn agony. But that Jane's knowledge of falling in love, her knowledge of Fanny Price, Emma Woodhouse, and Anne Elliot, was purely 'intuitive' may well be doubted. It is certain that the letters from Bath and Southampton have not the gusto of the earlier, nor the serenity of the later, letters. And some explanation is wanted of the long eclipse of her creative powers. We cannot hope to know the cause; but we are free to guess.

[1] Ch. 2.
[2] *Quarterly Review* 1821.

VI

CHAWTON: 1809-17

UNLIKE Steventon Rectory, Chawton Cottage is intact. It stood at the junction of the main road from London to Winchester and Southampton with the road to Gosport, and so afforded a view of the busy world, and particularly of post-chaises travelling to and from Winchester, bearing nephews and others—'future Heroes, Legislators, Fools and Villains'.[1] It was less than fifty miles from Hyde Park Corner, so that, in default of a brother's carriage, the journey could be made in a day by Yalden's Coach.[2] Within two miles was the town of Alton, where was the Alton bank, Austen Gray and Vincent, which was much the same thing as Austen Maunde and Tilson. Letters from Henrietta Street came to Alton 'by the parcel', and so to Chawton 'by favour of Mr. Gray'. Communication with Steventon was by lanes impassable to carriages; but James or Edward[3] would ride over; and letters

[1] Letter 130.
[2] Letter 99.
[3] James Edward Austen (Leigh); but he was called Edward, and has to be distinguished from his uncle Edward and his cousin 'little Edward' (who presently turn into Knights).

could be sent 'by the cheese',[1] or by the intercourse of Steventon Digweeds with Alton Digweeds.

Little remains of the improvements by which Edward Austen added comfort and dignity to his mother's home. The house had probably been an inn, and was large enough for the improver's hand.

A good-sized entrance and two sitting-rooms made the length of the house, all intended originally to look upon the road, but the large drawing-room window was blocked up and turned into a book-case, and another opened at the side which gave to view only turf and trees, as a high wooden fence and hornbeam hedge shut out the Winchester road. . . . There was a pleasant irregular mixture of hedgerow, and gravel walk, and orchard, and long grass for mowing, arising from two or three little enclosures having been thrown together.[2]

Less than half a mile from the Cottage was the Great House,[3] where Jane would again be able to 'sit in idleness in a well-proportioned room'. It was let to John Middleton, who introduces one of Jane's indirect contacts with the great world. Middleton was a widower, whose wife had been a Beckford of Basing and cousin of the author of *Vathek*. Jane does not mention William Beckford, but his cousin,

[1] Letter 130.

[2] *Memoir*, ch. 4. For the accommodation of the house see Letter 72 and my note there.

[3] For an account of this beautiful house see *Chawton Manor and its Owners*.

Middleton's sister-in-law Maria Beckford, was known to her at Chawton and in Welbeck Street, and she writes familiarly of Beckford's daughters.

This tenancy ended in 1812, and thereafter the Great House was often occupied for part of the year by Edward or by Frank, with their families. Later the Frank Austens established themselves at Alton, and Anna Austen, who had been a frequent visitor at the Cottage, lived near Alton after her marriage.

But for the present there was little society to tempt the ladies, who had no great wish to be tempted. We hear of the bachelor rector and his sister, of a naval officer and his wife and her relations, of the Rector of Faringdon and his enormous family; but we hear no more than politeness demanded. Some comedy was provided by Mr. Harry Digweed and his wife, links with Steventon, and by a very poor Miss Benn to whom it was proper to show kindness.

The Cottage had one frequent visitor. Charles Austen had married in Bermuda. In 1811 he came home, and presently was appointed to the *Namur*, the guardship at the Nore. There was difficulty in disposing of his little girls, even before his wife's death in 1814. We find them with her relations in London, and the eldest, 'that puss Cassy', was very often at Chawton.

Our first indication that Jane Austen was at last, after so long an interval, beginning again to think of publication as possible is furnished by a transaction which took place just before she left Southampton. She preserved among her papers a 'copy of a letter to Messrs Crosbie & Co and Mr. Crosbie's reply'.[1] The copy is not in her hand, and its original may have been composed for her by Henry. The letter, which is dated 5 April 1809, states that in the spring of 1803 'a MS Novel in 2 vol. entitled Susan' had been sold to Crosby by a gentleman of the name of Seymour (this must be Henry's man of business) for £10; that early publication was stipulated for, but did not follow. The writer, who is herself the authoress, can only suppose the manuscript to have been lost; if so, she can supply a duplicate. She asks for an early reply 'to Mrs. Ashton Dennis, Post Office, Southampton'; if none is received, she shall feel at liberty to apply elsewhere. Mr. Richard Crosby's reply was brief. There was no engagement to publish. If the book is published elsewhere, proceedings will be taken to stop the sale. But he adds 'the MS shall be yours for the same as we paid for it'.

This offer was not accepted. The *Memoir* tells us that it was not till four novels had been published—that is, after the publication of *Emma* in December

[1] 67 and 67a.

1815—that Henry Austen[1] bought back the manuscript and copyright of *Northanger Abbey*. When he had done so, he informed Mr. Crosby that it was by the authoress of *Pride and Prejudice*. The author of the *Memoir* confused the history by stating that the manuscript was sold to a publisher in Bath—an error which begat more error. But the matter was cleared up in the *Life*,[2] and there can be no reasonable doubt that *Susan* is *Northanger Abbey*. When Jane Austen prepared the book for publication she wrote an *Advertisement*, in which she stated that it was finished in 1803, and that thirteen years had since passed. This fixes 1816 as the year in which the manuscript was ready for press. The *Advertisement* states also that the book after its sale in 1803 'was even advertised'; and the advertisement has been traced. A list of 'New and Useful Books published by Crosby & Co', printed in *Flowers of Literature* for 1801–2 (which appeared in 1803), includes

---

[1] So in the first edition; the second cautiously substitutes 'one of her brothers'.

[2] Ch. 13. See above, p. 44. Mrs. L. M. Ragg has suggested a reconciliation of the story of a sale in Bath with the known fact of the sale to Crosby of London. She points out (*Jane Austen in Bath*, 1938, p. 50) that one Cruttwell, a printer and bookseller in Bath, was associated with Crosby in publishing *The Trial of Mrs. Leigh Perrot* (1800). If, as is likely enough, Cruttwell and Crosby had a regular trade connexion, it is possible that the first overtures for *Susan* were in fact made in Bath.

'Susan; a Novel in 2 volumes'. *Susan* does not figure in subsequent lists of *Flowers of Literature*. Even in 1816 publication was not finally decided, and the title seems to have been in doubt. For in March 1817 she told her niece Fanny that 'Miss Catherine is put upon the Shelve for the present, and I do not know that she will ever come out'.[1]

The history of *Northanger Abbey* has a bearing on the question of the degree in which the early novels were revised for publication. The change of the heroine's name from Susan to Catherine may be accounted for by the publication in 1809 of an anonymous *Susan* in two volumes. It may have been connected with Jane's choice of that name for her own *Lady Susan*. But whatever the motive, the change suggests a more general revision. Jane clearly had the habit of copying and recopying. Mrs. Ashton Dennis in April 1809 could supply another copy.[2] But if the book was rewritten in 1816, the authoress did not feel that it was up to date. In the *Advertisement* she apologizes for 'those parts of the book which thirteen years have made comparatively obsolete. The public are entreated to bear in mind that thirteen years have passed since it was finished,

[1] Letter 141.

[2] 'From particular circumstances' she could not engage to do so before August. There was an interval of visits between leaving Southampton and settling at Chawton.

many more since it was begun, and that during that period, places, manners, books and opinions have undergone considerable changes.'

No such apology was thought necessary for *Sense and Sensibility* or *Pride and Prejudice*. But it cannot be inferred that those books were completely re-written. The cases were not similar. *Northanger Abbey*, as a satire on Mrs. Radcliffe and her school, was by 1816 somewhat *démodé*. As that could not be altered, it may not have seemed worth while to alter minor matters. But the other books had no such temporary reference to date them, and were as true to life in 1810 as in 1800. The authors of the *Life* may nevertheless be right in finding in *Northanger Abbey* the best example of Jane's early manner.

When Jane at last overcame her diffidence, and her financial fears or scruples,[1] her choice fell not on *Susan* nor on *First Impressions*, but on *Sense and Sensibility*. We do not know why she preferred it to *First Impressions*, which had been the family favourite, and which she must have known to be more entertaining. But *Sense and Sensibility*, in the form in which it left Steventon,[2] was the later work;

---

[1] 'She actually made a reserve from her very moderate income to meet the expected loss.' *Biographical Notice*.
[2] For the earlier draft see p. 42.

and she may have feared that *First Impressions* would be thought frivolous.

We have no direct evidence on the question of revision. Henry Austen describes the novels first published as 'the gradual performances of her previous life'.[1] But in what follows he speaks not of revision, but of reluctance to admit the conviction that the books would do. 'Though in composition she was equally rapid and correct, yet an invincible distrust of her own judgement induced her to withhold her works from the public, till time and many perusals had satisfied her that the charm of recent composition was dissolved.' The *Memoir* has the rather vague expression 'rearranged and prepared for publication'.

The book itself supplies one piece of evidence which, though small, is definite, and one which is speculative. It has been pointed out that the mention of Cowper and Scott together, as popular poets, was impossible in 1798. The *Lay* was published in 1805, *Marmion* in 1808. Again, it is virtually certain that the title 'Pride and Prejudice' was taken from a passage in *Cecilia*. Now it seems probable that 'Sense and Sensibility' was modelled on 'Pride and Prejudice'; for the titles are of a type which had few precursors. If this is so, then *Sense and*

---

[1] *Biographical Notice.*

Sensibility was so named after 'Pride and Prejudice'
had been substituted for 'First Impressions'. But
this does not take us far.[1]

There is a break in the letters between July 1809,
the time of arrival at Chawton, and April 1811. By
that time Jane had made her decision to publish
Sense and Sensibility at her own expense, and was in
London with Henry, correcting proofs. Each of her
publications meant a visit to Henry, who seems to
have done all the business of negotiation. The
proofs might have been sent 'in the parcel' from
Henrietta Street to the bank at Alton; but this
would have caused delay, and perhaps loss of
anonymity. Moreover, Henry's literary advice
would be no less valued than his practical help.[2]

We know more about *Pride and Prejudice*, for we
have the author's own description of the process of
revision. 'I have lop'd and crop't so successfully

---

[1] Miss A. L. Tallmadge suggests that J. A. was thinking of
the well-known lines in Cowper's *Task* (1785: *The Winter Walk
at Noon*, 560):

> I would not enter on my list of friends
> (Though grac'd with polish'd manners and fine sense
> Yet wanting sensibility) the man
> Who needlessly sets foot upon a worm.

[2] The *Opinions* on *Mansfield Park* and *Emma* do not include
his. This cannot mean that they were compiled for his benefit;
for they contain opinions which he must have had from the
persons themselves. It must mean that his views were too well
known to J. A. to need record, or too detailed to admit it.

that I imagine it must be rather shorter than S. and S.'[1] This clearly refers to a recent operation.

A less certain criterion of the extent of the revision is supplied by a chronological test. In *Mansfield Park* and *Pride and Prejudice* particularly, the indications of time are numerous and precise, and have led to the conclusion that Jane Austen worked with a calendar. That she did so is antecedently probable; for her regard for accuracy in those parts of her work which belonged to the real and not to an ideal world was quite unlike that of authors in general. It is easy to believe her incapable of giving dates which could not have coexisted in the same year. And it would not appear possible to construct either of these two books without reference to a calendar, actual or ideal. If this is accepted, the inference is almost certain that *Pride and Prejudice* was constructed on the calendar of 1811-12, and was not merely rewritten, but very largely recast, in the year preceding publication.[2] It is not suggested that Jane intended to fix the book to a particular year; there is nothing in it which calls for

[1] Letter 76. The two books are of almost identical length.
[2] For the details of this inquiry—first carried out by Sir Frank MacKinnon—I must refer to my edition of the novels. The case for *Pride and Prejudice* is unfortunately embarrassed by an error on the author's part. But it is so gross an error that it must be ascribed to inadvertence; and there is a natural explanation of it.

precise dating. She does, however, write of her people as of contemporaries. When she went to a picture gallery to look for Mrs. Bingley and Mrs. Darcy, and was disappointed of Elizabeth, she not only saw a convincing Jane, but found her wearing the right clothes. 'She is dressed in a white gown, with green ornaments, which convinces me of what I had always supposed, that green was a favourite colour with her.'[1] She was not thinking of Jane in the very different costume of 1797.

There are, on the other hand, one or two elements which belong more properly to an earlier time. The Brighton militia camps of 1793–5 were famous; and they do not seem to have been repeated later. But the retention of the Brighton episode would not be felt as dating the story. There is also a reference to the Wickhams' 'manner of living' when (after the proper close of the book) 'the restoration of peace dismissed them to a home'. This might be anticipation; whether in 1797 or in 1812 a novelist might assume that the war would sometime end. But the reference might be to the peace of 1802; and this suggests a revision about 1803–4, when Jane was finishing *Susan* and probably writing *The Watsons*.

On the whole, it is difficult to resist the conclusion

[1] Letter 80.

that *Pride and Prejudice* is largely the work of its author's maturity. Yet it retains a youthful exuberance which the experienced spinster, nearing forty, could hardly recapture; and she seems to have felt this herself. When she writes, in 1813, of 'the playfulness and epigrammatism of the style', her tone is detached; she looks at her earlier work with affectionate admiration, contrasting it with the 'stupid' books she is now writing or intending to write.[1]

The chronology of the novels which were begun at Chawton is fixed by a memorandum made by the author and still extant:[2]

Mansfield Park. Begun somewhere about Feb^ry 1811. Finished soon after June 1813.

Persuasion. Begun Augt 8th 1815. Finished Augt 6th 1816.

Emma. Begun Jany 21 1814. Finished March 29 1815.

In the same letter[3] in which she reports the arrival of the first copy of *Pride and Prejudice*, Jane Austen writes:

Now I will try and write of something else, and it shall be a complete change of subject—ordination. I am

---

[1] Letter 77.

[2] Morgan Library. Facsimile in *Plan of a Novel*. Miss Thomson (*Survey*, p. 199) was mistaken in thinking that Henry invented the name *Persuasion*.

[3] Letter 76.

glad your enquiries have ended so well. If you could discover whether Northamptonshire is a country of Hedgerows I should be glad again.

Ordination can hardly be called the 'subject' of *Mansfield Park*; but the plot turns largely on Edmund Bertram's choice of a profession which did not suit Mary Crawford's ambitions. Cassandra's 'enquiries' we may suppose to be addressed to her brother James, with whom she was then staying, and to be concerned with the disposal of livings.[1]

But Jane's statement cannot mean what it seems to mean, that she was about to begin a new book. For we know from herself that *Mansfield Park* was begun two years earlier; and allusions in a letter written a few days before the letter just quoted show that Cassandra was already familiar with parts of the second volume.[2] The remarks on there being 'no Government House at Gibraltar' and on the 'round table at Mrs. Grant's' show that the career of William Price, and the intercourse between Mansfield Park and Mansfield Parsonage, were already developed.

The inquiry about hedgerows was serious. Jane

---

[1] *M.P.* ch. 3. James would be an authority on the ethical as well as the legal aspects of the matter, for he had declined to hold a living offered to him, from scruples about simony. *Life* 223.

[2] Letter 75.

had been born in a country of hedgerows, as the *Memoir* notes.[1]

The chief beauty of Steventon consisted in its hedge-rows. A hedgerow, in that country, does not mean a thin formal line of quickset, but an irregular border of copse-wood and timber, often wide enough to contain within it a winding footpath, or a rough cart-track. . . . Two such hedgerows radiated, as it were, from the parsonage garden.

The convenience of such hedgerows to a novelist is obvious, even if we had not read *Persuasion*. We may imagine that Fanny Price might have been the unwilling hearer of a conversation between Edmund and Mary, as Anne Elliot was of a tender passage between Wentworth and Louisa. But apparently the answer to Jane's inquiry was negative, and the idea had to be given up.

The topic of Northamptonshire is raised again in an unpublished letter to Martha Lloyd:[2]

I am obliged to you for your enquiries about Northamptonshire, but do not wish you to renew them, as I am sure of getting the intelligence I want from Henry.

We do not know what decided the choice of Northamptonshire. The scene of all the other novels is in counties which Jane knew well. But she wanted

---

[1] Ch. 2.   [2] 16 Feb. (1813). See p. 82.

a good hunting country—good enough to tempt
Henry Crawford—and one sufficiently remote from
Portsmouth to make Fanny's separation from her
family complete. The source of Jane's information
was guessed before the discovery of the letter last
quoted. Some years ago Sir Frank MacKinnon,
travelling in that county, made the acquaintance of
Cottesbrooke, and making up his mind[1] that it was
Mansfield Park, asked the editor of the *Letters* if
they had any mention of Langhams, baronets of that
place. I had to return a negative; but later I found
Sir James Langham in the *Opinions* of *Mansfield
Park* and *Emma*. Henry Austen had official duties
in Oxfordshire, and may have broken his journeys
at Cottesbrooke.

The letters of March 1814 show Jane's reliance
on Henry's help. He drove her from Chawton to
Henrietta Street, and when they were clear of Alton
they fell to work on the manuscript. The progress
of his reading and approbation is frequently reported
to Cassandra; 'I tell you all the good I can, as I
know how much you will enjoy it.' This was in the
first week of March, and the book was out before
the end of May. Two printers were employed, and

---

[1] Much as Henry Crawford, finding himself in a village in the
neighbourhood, 'told a man mending a hedge that it was
Thornton Lacey'. See *Times Lit. Suppl.* 10 and 31 Dec. 1931;
for Cottesbrooke itself, *Country Life*, 15 Feb. 1936.

were no doubt urged to dispatch as, two years later, were the printers of *Emma*. Jane could not leave London till the work was finished.

The amber cross which William Price brought home to his sister from Sicily[1] had its origin in Jane's affectionate remembrance of the 'gold chains and topaze crosses' which young Charles Austen, his prize-money burning his pocket, had sent his sisters from the Mediterranean in 1801.[2]

Soon after her return to Chawton Jane paid a visit to her cousins the Cookes at Bookham. She had, perhaps, already determined to 'take a heroine whom no one but myself will much like'.[3] While at Bookham she made or renewed acquaintance with the beauties of Boxhill, and at Leatherhead found the names 'Randalls' and 'Knightley'

By November 1814 *Mansfield Park* was sold out, and Jane paid a short visit to Henry with a view to a second edition. Her publisher, Egerton, seems to have hesitated; hence, perhaps, her decision to try another publisher. But we hear no more of the progress of *Emma* until, nearly a year later, Jane is in town again with a finished manuscript and is in negotiation with Mr. John Murray himself. The correspondence with him about terms and about

---

[1] *M.P.* ii, ch. 8.   [2] Letter 38.
[3] *Memoir*, ch. 10.

printing, and with the Prince Regent's librarian
about the Regent's gracious intimation that she was
'at liberty to dedicate any future work to H.R.H.',
is all very amusing; but it tells us nothing much of
the book itself. We do, however, learn that she was
diffident of the success of her masterpiece. When
she was writing *Mansfield Park* she had feared it
would be found 'not half so entertaining' as *Pride
and Prejudice*.[1] She was now afraid lest *Emma* fall
between two stools; 'I am strongly haunted with
the idea that to those readers who have preferred
Pride and Prejudice it will appear inferior in wit,
and to those who have preferred *Mansfield Park*
inferior in good sense.'[2]

The success of *Emma*, and the modest measure
of fame it brought her, did not make Jane less
cautious. As we have seen, she reversed the decision
of 1816 to publish 'Miss Catherine'; and though she
confessed to Fanny Knight in March 1817 that she
had 'a something ready for publication' she did not
then expect it to be published for 'about a twelve-
month'.[3] It appears from the next letter to Fanny
that Henry had been making inquiries, and that she
was afraid his sanguine views might be leading her
into rash courses.

---

[1] Letter 81.   [2] Letter 120.
[3] Letter 141. The something was *Persuasion*.

Do not be surprised at finding Uncle Henry acquainted with my having another ready for publication. I could not say No when he asked me, but he knows nothing more of it. You will not like it, so you need not be impatient. You may *perhaps* like the Heroine, as she is almost too good for me.[1]

The well-known story of the cancelled conclusion comes from the *Memoir*.[2]

The book had been brought to an end in July (1816); and the re-engagement of the hero and heroine effected in a totally different manner in a scene laid at Admiral Croft's lodgings. But her performance did not satisfy her. She thought it tame and flat, and was desirous of producing something better. This weighed upon her mind, the more so probably on account of the weak state of her health; so that one night she retired to rest in very low spirits. But such depression was little in accordance with her nature, and was soon shaken off. The next morning she awoke to more cheerful views and brighter inspirations; the sense of power revived; and imagination resumed its course. She cancelled the condemned chapter, and wrote two others, entirely different, in its stead.

But there were to be no more visits to London, or dealings with Mr. Murray. Nothing was done in Jane's lifetime.[3] Of *Sanditon* no more is known than that it was the work of her last months.

[1] Letter 142.   [2] Ch. 11.
[3] There is, of course, no reason to suppose that J. A. at any time contemplated publishing *Catherine* and *Persuasion* together.

The references in Jane Austen's letters to her art
and her books may be collected here.[1] The Steventon letters are disappointing; the two references to
First Impressions tell us no more than that it was
complete in manuscript; and the sentence 'an artist
cannot do anything slovenly' refers to another art—
she had been drawing to amuse a child.[2] The surviving letters of the Bath–Southampton period are
silent.

The Chawton letters show the excitements of publication, and give us glimpses of the fond yet critical
parent. *Pride and Prejudice* is 'my own darling
child', and there are references to heroines. Elinor
is 'my Elinor' (whom she hoped an acquaintance
would like), but there is nothing of Marianne. Her
joy in Elizabeth—'as delightful a creature as ever
appeared in print'—was probably never equalled.
There is no character of Catherine or Fanny. The
description of Emma as 'a heroine whom no one but
myself will much like' is not in any extant letter,
but is quoted in the *Memoir*.[3]

Apart from these descriptions the most interesting allusions are those to Henry Austen's progress
in the manuscript of *Mansfield Park*: his foreseeing

---

[1] My edition of the *Letters* collects all references to the novels
in Index VI, and indicates in Index IV the few comments on
novel-writing and literature generally.

[2] Letter 11 (1798).   [3] p. 157.

'how it will all be'; his liking Henry Crawford 'I
mean properly, as a clever, pleasant man'; his chang-
ing his mind, and defying 'any one to say whether
H. C. would be reformed, or would forget Fanny in
a fortnight'; his final approval of the conclusion.

In 1814 Jane Austen wrote a number of letters to
her niece Anna, who at one-and-twenty was engaged
on a novel. She wrote critically, though as to an
equal, and some of the criticisms are revealing, the
insistence especially on accuracy and consistency in
small matters.[1]

Her nephew and future biographer also tried his
hand, at eighteen. It is in a letter to him that the
famous 'little bit of ivory' is mentioned. Edward
had lost part of his manuscript, and his aunt pre-
tends to be under suspicion:

I do not think however that any theft of that sort
would be really very useful to me. What should I do
with your strong, manly, spirited Sketches, full of
Variety and Glow? How could I possibly join them on
to the little bit (two Inches wide) of Ivory on which I
work with so fine a Brush, as produces little effect after
much labour?[2]

[1] Letters, June–Dec. 1814.
[2] Letter 134.

VII

CHARACTER AND OPINIONS

HENRY AUSTEN thought even the few sentences that he was able to quote from his sister's letters 'more truly descriptive of her temper, tastes, feelings, and principles than anything which the pen of a biographer can produce'.[1] Many will agree with him. But the letters, as we shall find,[2] were deliberately robbed of much of their significance; and the surviving letters, like the novels but even more so, have given their readers impressions of the writer's character which are widely divergent. If we wish to know Jane Austen as she was, we are bound to consider the accounts of her by those who knew her. Allowance for family partiality and family loyalty may have to be made. But the sincerity and truthfulness of family portraits can be estimated; it is possible to distinguish the language of formal propriety from the language of loving enthusiasm.

The person who knew her best was the sister with whom, from childhood, she had lived in the closest possible intimacy. Cassandra Austen left no

---

[1] *Biographical Notice.*
[2] See p. 142.

character of Jane; but two letters have been preserved which she wrote to their favourite niece,
Fanny Knight, in the days after her loss.[1]

My dearest Fanny—doubly dear to me now for her
dear sake whom we have lost.

She did love you most sincerely, and never shall I
forget the proofs of love you gave her during her illness
in writing those kind, amusing letters at a time when I
know your feelings would have dictated so different a
style. . . .

I *have* lost a treasure, such a Sister, such a friend as
never can have been surpassed,—she was the sun of my
life, the gilder of every pleasure, the soother of every
sorrow, I had not a thought concealed from her, and it
is as if I had lost a part of myself. I loved her only too
well, not better than she deserved, but I am conscious
that my affection for her made me sometimes unjust to
and negligent of others, and I can acknowledge, more
than as a general principle, the justice of the hand which
has struck this blow. . . .

When I asked her if there was any thing she wanted,
her answer was that she wanted nothing but death and
some of her words were 'God grant me patience, Pray
for me oh Pray for me.' . . . I hope I do not break your
heart my dearest Fanny by these particulars. . . . I know
that you will apply to the fountain-head for consolation
and that our merciful God is never deaf to such prayers
as you will offer. . . .

---

[1] These will be found in *Brabourne*, ii. 333, and in *Letters*
(1932), ii. 503.

Her dear remains are to be deposited in the cathedral —it is a satisfaction to me to think that they are to lie in a Building she admird so much—her precious soul I presume to hope reposes in a far superior Mansion. May mine one day be reunited to it. . . .

My dearest Fanny

I have just read your letter for the third time, and thank you most sincerely for every kind expression to myself, and still more warmly for your praises of her who I believe was better known to you than to any human being besides myself. . . .

Never was human being more sincerely mourned by those who attended her remains than was this dear creature. May the sorrow with which she is parted with on earth be a prognostic of the joy with which she is hailed in heaven! . . .

Of course those employments suit me best which leave me most at leisure to think of her I have lost, and I do think of her in every variety of circumstance. In our happy hours of confidential intercourse, in the cheerful family party which she so ornamented, in her sickroom, on her death-bed, and as (I hope) an inhabitant of heaven.

From the chorus of disappointment and hostility with which some of our Intellectuals greeted the republication of the *Letters*, I select as representative an article by Mr. Harold Nicolson. Mr. Nicolson found the letters 'much worse than dull and trivial'. They are 'a desert of family gossip', revealing an 'appalling gentility of style and aspect', a wit 'old-maidish and disagreeable', a mind 'like a very small, sharp pair of scissors'. He was anxious to avoid, if he might, the recoil of this impression on his very different estimate of the novels, and concluded that the discrepancy is the result of accident. The letters do Jane injustice for various reasons, the chief of which is that most of them were written to Cassandra, who was 'as a woman, immeasurably dull'. He quotes from her letter to Fanny the sentences about Jane's burial in Winchester Cathedral —'her precious soul, I presume to hope, reposes in a far superior Mansion'—and draws the confident inference: 'Clearly Cassandra was not the sort of correspondent who would infuse ardours of fancy into a sister's pen.' This is significant. The sentence he quotes is sufficient in itself to condemn its writer. Her language is not the language of faith and humility, but the language of hypocrisy[1] or stupidity. This assumption betrays a want of historical perspective, which comes strangely from a trained diplomat, an accomplished historian, a weekly stylist.[2]

[1] Mr. E. M. Forster calls it sanctimoniousness. *Times Lit. Suppl.* 10 Nov. 1932. See p. 108.

[2] Some such expression of pious hope was, of course, inevitable in such a letter. Examples could easily be multiplied; I content myself with a remark of Scott's in a letter announcing

When we turn to Henry Austen's *Notice* of his sister, we know we have to be on our guard—for Jane herself has warned us[1]—against his 'brotherly vanity and love'. But his eulogy of 'those endowments which sweetened every hour of her friends' lives' compels our attention:

If there be an opinion current in the world, that perfect placidity of temper is not reconcileable to the most lively imagination, and the keenest relish for wit, such an opinion will be rejected for ever by those who have had the happiness of knowing the author of the following works. Though the frailties, foibles, and follies of others could not escape her immediate detection, yet even on their vices did she never trust herself to comment with unkindness. The affectation of candour[2] is not uncommon, but she had no affectation. Faultless herself, as nearly

his brother's death; 'He had been long so very unwell that death was only a release to him and as I hope and trust an exchange for a better place.' *Letters*, ed. Grierson, iv. 245. Such phrases were, indeed, 'common form'. That does not prove them insincere or unintelligent. Miss Lascelles, when she read my manuscript many years ago, made this comment: 'Cassandra was brought up on Johnson, and said exactly what she meant—e.g. in "I presume to hope". But Mr. Nicolson (and probably other, less articulate, readers) hear this as an empty phrase, the words having stuck together in the oil of Dickens's humbugs. No one who fails to recognize such linguistic changes ought to poise critical opinions on single phrases.'

[1] See p. 131.

[2] The word has changed meaning; but we have Jane's own definition of it: 'candour without ostentation or design—to take the good of everybody's character, and make it still better, and say nothing of the bad.' *P. & P.* i. 4.

as human nature can be, she always sought, in the faults
of others, something to excuse, to forgive or forget.
When extenuation was impossible, she had a sure refuge
in silence. She never uttered either a hasty, a silly, or a
severe expression. . . .

One trait only remains to be touched on. It makes all
others unimportant. She was thoroughly religious and
devout; fearful of giving offence to God, and incapable
of feeling it towards any fellow creature. On serious
subjects she was well-instructed, both by reading and
meditation, and her opinions accorded strictly with those
of our Established Church.

The last sentence provokes a smile. But in 1817
there was no bathos in concluding a character with
a certificate of orthodoxy.

Her nephew, exploring fifty years later his own
affectionate memory, draws a picture which is more
impressive because it is less rhetorical.[1]

I can indeed bear witness that there was scarcely a
charm in her most delightful characters that was not a
true reflection of her own sweet temper and loving
heart. I was young when we lost her; but the impressions made on the young are deep, and though in the
course of fifty years I have forgotten much, I have not
forgotten that 'Aunt Jane' was the delight of all her
nephews and nieces. We did not think of her as being
clever, still less as being famous; but we valued her as
one always kind, sympathizing, and amusing. To all

[1] *Memoir*, chs. 1, 4, 5; pp. 2, 82, 90–2, 176 in my edition.

this I am a living witness, but whether I can sketch out such a faint outline of this excellence as shall be perceptible to others may be reasonably doubted.

Before the Austens left Southampton, when Jane's nephew was ten years old, he visited them there, and 'now began to know, and, what was the same thing, to love her'. He quotes her nieces:

As a very little girl I was always creeping up to aunt Jane and following her whenever I could, in the house and out of it. I might not have remembered this but for the recollection of my mother's telling me privately, that I must not be troublesome to my aunt. Her first charm to children was great sweetness of manner. She seemed to love you, and you loved her in return.[1]

As I grew older, when the original seventeen years between our ages seemed to shrink to seven, or to nothing, it comes back to me how strangely I missed her. It had become so much a habit with me to put by things in my mind with a reference to her, and to say to myself, I shall keep this for aunt Jane.[2]

A nephew of hers used to observe that his visits to Chawton, after the death of his aunt Jane, were always a disappointment to him. From old association he could not help expecting to be particularly happy in that house; and never till he got there could he realise to

[1] Caroline Austen.
[2] Anna Austen. She was born in April 1793, her aunt in December 1775.

himself how all its peculiar charm was gone. . . . The chief light in the house was quenched.[1]

She was buried in Winchester Cathedral. . . . Her own family alone attended the funeral. Her sister returned to her desolated home, there to devote herself, for ten years, to the care of her aged mother; and to live much in the memory of her lost sister, till called many years later to rejoin her. Her brothers went back sorrowing to their several homes. They were very fond and very proud of her. They were attached to her by her talents, her virtues, and her engaging manners; and each loved afterwards to fancy a resemblance in some niece or daughter of his own to the dear sister Jane, whose perfect equal they yet never expected to see.[2]

We have two contemporary accounts from outside the family. One is by Fulwar William Fowle, who was Martha Lloyd's nephew though not related to the Austens, and had met Jane at Southampton when he was a boy at Winchester. In 1870 he wrote to Caroline Austen:

Your dear Aunt Jane I can testify to as being the attractive, animated, delightful person her Biographer has represented her. . . . The last time I ever saw her was at Steventon, when she was on a visit to your Mother. . . . She was a very sweet reader. She had just

[1] This, though stated impersonally, seems to be the biographer's own experience.

[2] *Memoir*, ch. 11.

H

finished the first Canto of Marmion. . . . When Mr. W. Digweed was announced it was like the interruption of some pleasing dream.

The other witness is the obscure Mrs. Barrett.[1]

There is one fragment more which I would willingly linger on and expand—the tribute of my old friend to the real and true spring of religion which was always present though never obtruded. Miss Austen, she used to say, had on all the subjects of enduring religious feeling the deepest and strongest convictions, but a contact with loud and noisy exponents of the then popular religious phase made her reticent almost to a fault. She had to suffer something in the way of reproach from those who believed she might have used her genius to greater effect; but her old friend used to say 'I think I see her now defending what she thought was the real province of a delineator of life and manners, and declaring her belief that example and not "direct preaching" was all that a novelist could properly afford to exhibit'. Mrs. Barrett used to add 'Anne Elliot was herself; her enthusiasm for the navy, and her perfect unselfishness, reflect her completely'.

These stories are remarkable in their unanimity and in their character. Between those who are able to accept them as true, and those to whom Jane Austen has revealed herself in her letters as a trivial, narrow, snobbish, cold, and ill-bred woman, there can be no common ground. Mr. Nicolson's com-

[1] See p. 127.

promise will not hold water; if Jane Austen was not an odious woman, she could not have written odious letters to her sister.

Is any compromise possible? If, as some have thought, Jane Austen was a woman of sterling character and strong family attachments, but of a repellent personality—worldly, censorious, and hard —it is possible that her genius might have promoted the growth of a family legend about her, which would have softened her asperities and made the most of her sterner virtues and her intellectual gifts. But this family story is in fact unlike a legend concocted by interest or vanity. It reads like the spontaneous expression of genuine affection; and the quality which it throws into high relief is not so much the virtue, moral or intellectual, of its subject, as her charm—her unfailing good humour, her animation and enthusiasm, the flow of her sympathy. The metaphors which come naturally into the writers' minds are those of sweetness and sunshine. Her nephews and nieces, young as they were, remembered her as the light and joy of their lives; and in their old age the beloved aunt was still more to them than the famous writer.

We label her a social satirist, and her books a comedy of manners. She herself, very naturally, emphasized the comic aspect of her work, as when

she declared that if she had to write a serious romance to save her life, and might never relax into
laughing at herself or at other people, she should be
hung before she finished the first chapter.[1] We
recall Elizabeth Bennet's confession,[2] and the incomparable gallery of fools. But the observation
and record of folly and meanness and pretence,
though it may be thought her most conspicuous
talent, does not explain her hold on our affections.
Her books, with all their variety of excellence, are
unpretentious love-stories. It is the interest of the
stories, and of the young people whose happiness
they involve, that makes its confident appeal to
every generation of young readers.[3] Jane's own
affections centred in her young people, and especially, of course, in her heroines. 'Her liking Darcy
and Elizabeth is enough, she might hate all the
others if she would';[4] 'I must confess that I think
her (Elizabeth) as delightful a creature as ever

[1] Letter 126.
[2] 'I hope I never ridicule what is wise or good. Follies and
nonsense, whims and inconsistencies *do* divert me, I own, and I
laugh at them whenever I can.'
[3] The author of the *Memoir* (ch. 7) describes the 'mystic
process' of Jane's composition as that whereby 'Fanny Price, or
Emma Woodhouse or Anne Elliot was growing into beauty and
interest'. Here, as elsewhere, that unassuming critic showed a
true sense of proportion.
[4] Letter 78.

appeared in print';[1] and we are willing to agree.
Yet Elizabeth, and her sisters of the other novels,
are not in any way remarkable, except that we like
them enough to make their names household words,
and seem to know them so well that we hardly think
of them as born in George the Third's reign. Their
simple virtues, the charm of their youth and good
looks and happy natures, are matters of everyday
experience. The power which makes them live is
rare indeed. Jane Austen's 'talent for describing the
involvements and feelings of ordinary life' seemed
to Walter Scott 'the most wonderful I ever met
with'.[2] The secret of enduring fiction is sympathy
and passion—an emotional not an intellectual en-
dowment. That, and that alone, can make 'ordinary
commonplace things and characters interesting from
the truth of the description and the sentiment'.[3] But
imaginative sympathy demands an abundant share
of the qualities on which it is exercised. If we are to
make Jane Austen's achievement credible, we must
not hesitate to allow her largeness of soul. To think
of her as a hard and narrow spinster is to fashion a
chimera.

If we believe the account of Jane Austen's character that has been handed down, we shall be able to

---

[1] Letter 76.   [2] *Journal*, 14 March 1826.
[3] Scott's *Journal*, loc. cit.

form some idea of the author of *Persuasion*. We shall think of her as richly endowed: a woman of great vitality, of generous impulses, of a large-hearted charity; gifted, in a pre-eminent degree, with that power of intuitive sympathy in which women excel. We shall think that she expresses herself when she tells us that Anne Elliot 'prized the frank, the open-hearted, the eager character beyond all others. Warmth and enthusiasm did captivate her still. She felt that she could so much more depend upon the sincerity of those who sometimes looked or said a careless or a hasty thing, than of those whose presence of mind never varied, whose tongue never slipped';[1] and when she makes Emma exclaim 'There is no charm equal to tenderness of heart. . . . Dear Harriet! I would not change you for the clearest-headed, longest-sighted, best-judging female breathing.'[2]

Such a nature and such powers, however extraordinary in their degree, could not have done what Jane Austen did, if they had not been directed and controlled by consummate artistic gifts; but without them mere artistry would have worked in vain. Her wealth of sympathy is in fact not reserved for the prime objects of her affection, but is liberally extended to the objects of her ridicule. Even in real

[1] *Persuasion* ii. 6. [2] *Emma* ii. 13.

life she could love a fool. 'Dear Mrs. Digweed!',
she exclaims, 'I cannot bear that she should not be
foolishly happy after a Ball.' Scott was wrong, I
must believe, in saying that 'Characters of folly or
simplicity, such as those of old Woodhouse[1] and
Miss Bates, are ridiculous when first presented, but
if too often brought forward or too long dwelt upon,
their prosing is apt to become as tiresome in fiction
as in real society.' But Mr. Woodhouse does not
tire us, for all his absurdity; we bear with him, as
Emma bore with him, and for the same reason. His
kindly solicitude—'My dear, did you change your
stockings?'—delights us as it delighted Jane Fairfax. Miss Bates 'is a woman that one may, that one
must laugh at',[2] and the consummate art of her great
speeches makes them exquisitely laughable. But
we never lose patience with her; Emma's cruelty to
her is the most painful thing in a book which has
few painful moments.[3]

If there are apparent discrepancies between the
character of Jane Austen which is suggested by
trustworthy record and seems to be consonant
with the nature of her works, and other evidence supplied by her letters, it is the historian's

---

[1] We do not permit ourselves to say 'old Lear', or even 'old
Harding' (the Warden in the Barchester novels).

[2] *Emma* ii. 12.

[3] Miss Thomson is admirable on this. *Survey* 189.

business to examine these discrepancies and if possible to solve them. The inquiry has, in fact, seldom been conducted with much regard to historical method.

One reason why the letters have disappointed many readers is obvious enough. It is that they went to them with unreasonable expectations. Having enjoyed the novels, they opened the letters with high hopes of entertainment, only to find them made up of family news, mostly commonplace and largely meaningless. Some readers are never disappointed. But that is because they have thought it worth while to acquaint themselves with the family history, and so to put themselves, as far as may be, into Cassandra's place. It was, and is, a very attractive family. Then it all becomes interesting enough to be read with attention; and as we attend, we are rewarded by the turn of a phrase; we catch an inflection, or share an emotion. We do not demand such nicety of appreciation from the rapid and ignorant reader; we are content that, if he is not amused, he shall remember that he had no right to expect family gossip to be very amusing. But that many readers have been not only bored, but unwarrantably resentful, appears from the injustice of their complaints. One critic[1] complains loudly of 'her constant pre-

---

[1] Mr. Nicolson. Contrast Mr. David Garnett: 'the things

occupation with unimportant topics and with un-
interesting people, which leaves upon the mind this
glum impression of almost silliness'. He quotes in
justification two sentences: 'I intended to call on the
Miss Biggs yesterday had the weather been toler-
able.' 'I have determined to trim my lilac sarsenet
with black satin ribbon, just as my China Crape is,
6d. width at the bottom, 3d. or 4d. at top.' The
Misses Bigg were Jane's and Cassandra's dear friends,
and the gratuitous assumption that they were un-
interesting people shows that the critic is out of
temper. There can be nothing silly in telling a sister
that rain has prevented one from paying a call. And
do we need to read Jane Austen's letters to learn
that ladies are interested in details of dress? If
Cassandra was prepared to pay sixpence or more for
such communications, that is her affair, and there is
no more to be said.[1]

But there are many complaints against the letters
which cannot be dismissed as due to mere inatten-
tion or natural disappointment. There are passages
which have been thought to justify, or to require,
a very unfavourable judgement of the writer's

which one sister has always written to another', *Saturday Review
of Literature*, 14 Jan. 1933.

[1] 'I shall now try to write only what is necessary . . . so expect
a vast deal of small matter concisely told.' Letter 66.

character. It would be impossible to examine all
the charges, but a few may be chosen.

Mr. Forster[1] invites his readers to walk in the
rectory garden and to guess what is wrong: 'Can
it be the drains?' He is horrified by the 'deplorable
lapses of taste' shown in Miss Austen's 'comments
on expectant motherhood'. The passages referred to
are those in which she frankly admits the evidence
of her eyes, and uses the word 'big' in the sense
then current. This is no doubt distressing to a
sensitive middle-aged bachelor; I notice that women
are less squeamish. But all the critics, I believe,
who have noticed it are shocked by one passage in
an early letter:

> Mrs. Hall, of Sherborne, was brought to bed yester-
> day of a dead child, some weeks before she expected,
> owing to a fright. I suppose she happened unawares
> to look at her husband.[2]

Mr. Forster hears in this sally 'the whinny-
ing of harpies'. It is, no doubt, a naughty joke,
and shockingly unladylike. Miss Jane Austen of
Chawton would not have allowed herself to be
amused by such a thought. But it is a privilege
claimed by youth to abstract the comic aspect of a
situation from its other aspects. If that is heartless,
young people *are* heartless. Many of us, I imagine,

---

[1] *T.L.S.* 10 Nov. 1932.   [2] Letter 10 (Oct. 1798).

would be glad to feel sure that the letters of our early twenties contained no worse ribaldry than this.[1]

The same writer draws a picture, as brilliant as it is unpleasant, of the young Jane, taking her fun where she found it.

Lydia Bennet is all pervading: balls, officers, giggling, dresses, officers, balls, fill sheet after sheet until every one except Kitty grows weary. . . . The young girl dances and her eyes sparkle duly, but they are observant and hard; officers, dances, officers, giggling, balls.

The details of the picture might be challenged. There are in fact very few officers at these balls, and I recall nothing that can fairly be called a giggle. But let that pass; the general impression is what matters. It may be admitted that the Steventon Jane is harder than the Chawton Jane; nearer to Elizabeth and Emma than to Fanny and Anne. Elizabeth could appreciate her sister's candour, but did not pretend that she had it. It was not in Jane Austen's nature to think people better or wiser than they were. She faced realities even so far as to 'flatter herself she had a good eye for an adulteress'.[2]

---

[1] I once ventured to put this test case to an audience of young women. It was received, not with the pained silence I was prepared for, but with a shout of merriment.

[2] Letter 36; this was, of course, suppressed by the first editor.

But to say that the early letters were written by Lydia is to say that Jane was Lydia, and to forget that in these very years she created Elizabeth. This is impossible; for though Elizabeth knew all about Lydia, Lydia could know nothing of Elizabeth.[1]

Jane Austen's critics have said very little of her religion, being for the most part content to assume that she had none, or none that mattered. It is clear that she went to church; but that is dismissed as customary observance. We know also that she read sermons: 'I am very fond of Sherlock's Sermons, prefer them to almost any.'[2] This suggests more than customary observance; Sherlock was born in the seventeenth century, and his sermons cannot have been the ordinary reading of ladies in the nineteenth. She read also her cousin Edward Cooper's, and did not like them, finding them too full, for her taste, of regeneration and conversion and the Bible Society. Henry said that she was 'well-instructed on serious subjects, both by reading and meditation'; and if that is true it is significant,

---

[1] 'Miss Austen and Jane Austen.' Mr. E. M. Forster (*et tu, Brute!*) has acknowledged this, and earlier articles on the novels and fragments, which he collected in *Abinger Harvest*, 1936. Like Mr. Nicolson, he professes still to be a lover of Jane Austen the novelist, but cannot recognize her in the drab letter-writer. This dualism is not a workable theory; a harpy does not change her spots.

[2] Letter 101 (1814).

for we cannot believe that she devoted study and meditation to subjects which did not interest her.[1]

Her lack of interest in religious subjects has been inferred from the paucity of references to them in her letters. But if we accept the contemporary description of her reticence, we shall not expect much religion in her letters; certainly not in her extant letters. That 'in the letters written from Hans Place there is more talk of dress and shopping, of parties, theatres and picture galleries, than of sermons and preachers' should surprise no one, though it has distressed Miss Thomson.[2] But in fact there are, in the extant letters, references to the efficacy of 'religious principle', and of the sacrament;[3] simple, matter-of-fact statements. Should they be regarded as merely conventional?

One passage has specially vexed the critics—a reference to the death of Sir John Moore.[4]

I am sorry to find that Sir J. Moore has a mother living, but tho' a very Heroick son, he might not be a very necessary one to her happiness. Deacon Morrell may be more to Mrs. Morrell. I wish Sir John had united something of the Christian with the hero in his death.

[1] Two prayers composed by her have survived in manuscript. See p. 165.   [2] *Survey*, p. 275.

[3] See Index IV in my edition of the *Letters*.

[4] Letter 66. See my note there.

The key to this is partly lost. We know who Morrell was, but nothing of his relation to his mother, and therefore we cannot guess what was in Jane's mind. But we know a good deal about Sir John's death-bed, which was fully reported. He showed concern about public opinion at home, and sent messages to his friends. But it was not reported that he made any profession of faith. Mr. Forster quotes this passage with no further comment than to ascribe its spirit to Sir Thomas Bertram; he thinks, that is, that it stands self-condemned. Miss Thomson[1] is more precise. She has satisfied herself that we 'cannot believe that Jane Austen's creed was a vital and inspiring thing', partly on the ground that there is little about religion in the letters. She feels bound therefore to weigh this exceptional passage, which 'might be taken to imply religious feeling'. Her conclusion is that it is 'not only conventional, but an offence against good taste', and even 'singularly *banal*'; for 'no Christian could have died more nobly'. An advocate might plead that it is hard if Jane Austen must be convicted of indifference by her silence and of bad taste when she breaks it. What she says does not detract from the nobility of Moore's heroic death; she regrets, as a Christian, that so noble a

[1] *Survey*, p. 275.

hero did not, in his end, testify to his faith. Her critic's language betrays the assumption that orthodoxy is in itself '*banal*'. But in 1809 orthodoxy was not yet afraid to claim universal adherence as of right. To introduce questions of good taste is an anachronism.

This is not the place to inquire what their religion meant to ordinary orthodox people of the early nineteenth century, nor how far they meant by religion what we should rather call morals. It was admittedly not an age of religious ferment. But it was an age in which religious observance took up a great deal of people's time, and of their thoughts. It is impossible to suppose that the practice of religion, by good and thoughtful people, was either insincere or merely formal.[1] Yet Jane Austen's critics often write as if the clergymen she depicts, and their counterparts in real life, were, if not insincere, at least perfunctory in their religious beliefs and practice. 'Where any one body of educated men', Edmund Bertram remarks, 'are condemned indiscriminately, there must be a deficiency of information, or (smiling) of something else.'[2] And if Jane Austen acquiesces, as in part she

[1] Archdeacon Grantly was a worldly man. But he was quite sincere in thinking that there was 'more true religion' in his diocese before Mrs. Proudie and Mr. Slope spoiled the Cathedral services and introduced the Sabbath.   [2] p. 110.

does, in the practices of pluralism, non-residence, and the treatment of the Church as a profession for the younger sons of gentlemen, we may agree that she was not, so far, a religious reformer, but we must not infer that she was irreligious or morally obtuse. What she knew and recorded was, as her biographer says, 'the opinions and practice then prevalent among respectable and conscientious clergymen before their minds had been stirred, first by the Evangelical, and afterwards by the High Church movement'.[1]

The idea of the Church as a profession like others is naturally repugnant to the modern conscience. But allowance should be made for the conditions of a different age. In Jane Austen's time the orthodoxy of even educated people might in general be assumed. The clergyman was little troubled by his own doubts or by those of others. The Church as a whole had, as always, to contend with the world and the flesh; but it was not much called upon to fight scepticism without or to search its own conscience.

Again, in the rural England which Jane Austen knew, economic changes had not created the problems which afterwards became formidable.[2] Her

---

[1] *Memoir*, ch. 10.

[2] We may except great cities and the neglected industrial poor, which her experience hardly touched.

clergymen were village clergymen. There is nothing to shock us in the view that a young man of fair ability and good character, who like Edmund Bertram had 'no natural disinclination', might be a good parish priest without any special vocation.

Jane Austen's attitude to religious matters was not, in fact, that of simple acceptance. Her considered opinion of the duties of a clergyman is not that of *Northanger Abbey* but that of *Mansfield Park*, which shows that she had given thought to the matter of residence, and shared Sir Thomas Bertram's view that a

parish has wants and claims which can be known only by a clergyman constantly resident, and which no proxy can be capable of satisfying to the same extent. Edmund might, in the common phrase, do the duty of Thornton, that is, he might read prayers and preach, without giving up Mansfield Park; he might ride over, every Sunday, to a house nominally inhabited, and go through divine service; he might be the clergyman of Thornton Lacey every seventh day, for three or four hours, if that would content him. But it will not. He knows that human nature needs more lessons than a weekly sermon can convey, and that if he does not live among his parishioners and prove himself by constant attention their well-wisher and friend, he does very little either for their good or his own.[1]

[1] *Mansfield Park*, p. 248.

Jane was aware that her portraits of the clergy were not everywhere approved. Mr. Sherer, the good vicar at Godmersham, she notes, was 'displeased with my picture of clergymen'; and a lady 'thought it wrong, in times like these, to draw such clergymen as Mr. Collins and Mr. Elton'.[1] But *Mansfield Park* was generally praised for its good sense and its morality. Jane's cousins the Cookes

admire 'Mansfield Park' exceedingly. Mr. Cooke says 'it is the most sensible novel he ever read', and the manner in which I treat the clergy delights them very much.[2]

The Cookes were thoughtful people, perhaps of evangelical leanings.[3] They welcomed *Mansfield Park* as a protest against lax views of the clerical duty.

Jane's own attitude to the religious controversy of her time appears from slight indications. In 1809 she was disinclined to read Hannah More's *Coelebs* —'I do not like the Evangelicals'. But she added that 'Of course I shall be delighted, when I read it, like other people.'[4] A few years later she confessed a doubt, and advised her niece not to reject a suitor

---

[1] *Opinions* of *Emma*.   [2] Letter 96.

[3] *Memoir*, ch. 4. George Cooke, Jane's contemporary, was a noted tutor of Corpus. He became the teacher of Arnold and Keble, and 'an impressive preacher of earnest awakening sermons'.

[4] Letter 65.

on the ground of excessive virtue. 'Do not be frightened from the connection by your Brothers having most wit. Wisdom is better than Wit, & in the long run will certainly have the laugh on her side; & don't be frightened by the idea of his acting more strictly up to the precepts of the New Testament than others.' She and her niece differed about the meaning of the word evangelical; but 'I am by no means convinced that we ought not all to be Evangelicals, & am at least persuaded that they who are so from Reason and Feeling, must be happiest and safest.'[1] This is not the language of apathy.

The common opinion that Jane Austen never raised her eyes from the village scene and was indifferent to national affairs is a wholly unwarrantable inference from the artistic economy of her novels and the domestic nature of her extant letters. It is incompatible with her serious reading[2] and with the breadth of her outlook and the accuracy of her information; of which the indications, though slight, are sufficient. She read the newspapers; and her gentlemen sometimes talk politics, though she knew better than to reproduce their conversation. She makes, perhaps, only one specific reference to

---

[1] Letters 103, 106 (410, 420).

[2] Witness her youthful zeal for the Stuart cause, and her mature enthusiasm for Capt. Pasley's *Military Policy and Institutions of the British Empire*.

patriotic sentiment, but it is emphatic. Letters
written from abroad, she confessed, 'would not be
satisfactory to *me* unless they breathed a strong
spirit of regret for not being in England'.[1] Her
friend Mrs. Barrett, identifying her with Anne
Elliot, gave as their salient features 'perfect unselfishness' and 'enthusiasm for the navy'; and we
can make out that both Jane's and Anne's enthusiasm was based on exact knowledge.

Before we infer Jane's narrowness from her
silences, let us admit the possibility that she knew,
better than we can, how to get the results she aimed
at. The limits she imposed on herself were of her
own choice, and were narrower even than the limits
of her experience required. Though she had lived
in towns, and was not unacquainted with London,
she never chose an urban scene. It suited her sometimes to take her heroines to Bath or London; but
the rural background is always preserved. She had
set out to paint 'pictures of domestic life in country
villages'; 'three or four Families in a Country Village is the very thing to work on'.[2] She chose a
village, or a country house, because that was what
she knew and loved best.

Much could not be hoped from the traffic of even the
busiest part of Highbury;—Mr. Perry walking hastily

---

[1] Letter 139 (1817).   [2] Letter 126, 100.

by, Mr. William Cox letting himself in at the office door, Mr. Cole's carriage horses returning from exercise, or a stray letter-boy on an obstinate mule, were the liveliest objects she could presume to expect; and when her eyes fell only on the butcher with his tray, a tidy old woman travelling homewards from shop with her full basket, two curs quarrelling over a dirty bone, and a string of dawdling children round the baker's little bow-window eying the gingerbread, she knew she had no reason to complain, and was amused enough; quite enough still to stand at the door. A mind lively and at ease, can do with seeing nothing, and can see nothing that does not answer.[1]

Miss Thomson[2] calls this an admirable picture of 'the tedium of life in a country town'. But the significance of the picture is that Emma did not find it tedious.

Even within these limits Jane was rigorous in excluding everything that would not fit her design, everything of which she did not feel herself to be mistress. She hardly ever permits herself a male conversation without female audience; no doubt because she distrusted her powers. This restraint is very rare indeed, and it is part of her genius. But it has not always been understood.[3]

[1] *Emma*, p. 233.　　　　　[2] *Survey*, p. 257.
[3] She was perfectly aware that 'an essay on the history of Buonaparte' would have improved *P. & P.* by giving it greater variety. But she felt the sacrifice as inevitable.

One consequence is that her men, since they may not leave the drawing-room, can exhibit their more manly attributes only by indirect and allusive methods. William Price, like Othello, could plausibly be made to tell stories of his adventures. Captain Wentworth in talk with the Admiral could glance at the perils and hardships of the service. But with such sidelights we must be content.[1]

These lacunae in the lives of Jane Austen's young men have been variously regarded. Darcy, in particular, 'soars out of the picture; most of him happens off'.[2] This may be thought[3] to detract from

---

[1] Whether Jane's men are in fact convincingly masculine is a debatable point.

[2] I quote Miss Elizabeth Bowen; see p. 172.

[3] e.g. by Miss Lascelles, who aptly contrasts the continuity of Mr. Knightley, who, when he is not at Hartfield, is kept alive by William Larkins. The extreme nihilist view has been stated (in a private letter (ed. 1926, ii. 471), not *ex cathedra*) by Walter Raleigh in a characteristically capricious analysis of the young men in *Pride and Prejudice*: 'There is no scrap of evidence that they can *do* anything, shoot a partridge, or add up figures, or swim, or brush their hair.' There is, in fact, ample evidence on some of these heads. Jane Austen knew the delights and toils of hunting from the exploits of her younger brothers, which are reflected in William Price. Her acquaintance with shooting appears in Charles Musgrove's earnest attention to guns and vermin. I shall be surprised if Henry Tilney and Edmund Bertram were not competent arithmeticians. But my point is that for swimming and hair-brushing we ought not to expect any evidence. I doubt if Jane Austen had ever seen a grown man perform either of these exercises.

his substantiality. But it may be said that a Prince Charming is entitled to withdraw into the unknown from which he has romantically emerged. The extreme case, of course, is Psyche's ignorance of her Cupid. But even in England a landlord with a great rent roll, a serious and perhaps an ambitious young man, who might be asked to stand for the County, had connexions and occupations which were, in fact, remote from the experience of Longbourn.

Other possibilities, less remote, were even less open to exploration. 'She found his manners very pleasing indeed. The little flaw of his having a mistress now living with him at Ashdown Park, seems to be the only unpleasing circumstance about him.'[1] This side of life was not hidden from Jane Austen, or from other readers of *Tom Jones*; but convention forbade its recognition in a 'novel by a lady'. In the first edition of *Sense and Sensibility* Mrs. Jennings does mention a natural son; but this was expunged in the second.

Mention must be made of Miss Mitford, the first of the detractors. In 1870 A. G. L'Estrange published his *Life of Mary Russell Mitford*, in which he printed a letter from Miss Mitford, written in 1815.[2] In this letter Miss Mitford describes her mother's

---

[1] Letter 30.
[2] Vol. i, p. 305. *Life* 84, 300, gives the text.

recollection of the young Jane, whom she knew 'before her marriage', and quotes a contemporary account of Jane in later life. The author of the *Memoir*, published in the same year, permitted himself a dignified postscript,[1] in which he pointed out that Miss Mitford's mother was married in 1785, and had left the neighbourhood of Steventon early in 1783, when Jane was seven years old. He did not consider the second charge, 'because Miss Mitford candidly expresses a doubt whether she had not been misinformed'.

Thus the two familiar pictures—of the 'husband-hunting butterfly' and the 'poker of whom everyone is afraid'—are of more than doubtful authenticity; the first is anachronistic, and the second came from a poisoned source.[2] The resulting situation is not unsatisfactory. Those to whom it is congenial to think that Jane Austen began as a minx and ended as a 'perpendicular piece of single blessedness' will say that Miss Mitford's phrases are too apt to be the fruit of mere error. Those who choose to disbelieve her may do so with a clear conscience.

[1] He did not reprint it in his second edition.
[2] The sister-in-law of a man who was then at law with Edward Knight.

VIII

FACT AND FICTION

JANE AUSTEN was singularly scrupulous in her regard for accuracy in those parts of her fiction which were grounded on fact—such as dates and places. She would not trust herself in a county she did not know, at least by report; and advised her niece against adventures in Ireland. 'Let the Portmans go to Ireland, but as you know nothing of the Manners there, you had better not go with them. You will be in danger of giving false representations. Stick to Bath.'[1] She would not put a hedgerow in a county of which hedgerows were not a feature.[2] There is good reason to believe that in two at least of her books she worked with a calendar;[3] it is certain that, unlike the great majority of novelists, she took great pains to make her dates mutually consistent. In Bath, her theatres and concerts, her Upper Rooms and Lower Rooms, are always on the right days of the week. We can make out that the day on which Mrs. Bennet lamented that 'there is not a bit of fish to be got' was a Monday.[4]

---

[1] Letter 98.
[2] See p. 83.
[3] See p. 79.
[4] *Pride and Prejudice* i. 13.

But she is more than accurate. She clings to reality in a way which might argue poverty of invention, if that explanation were not absurd. She could not bring herself to invent the names of ships which she wanted for *Mansfield Park*, but asked her brother for leave to use some of his; though she was aware that in doing so she risked what was left of her anonymity.[1] Highbury is near Leatherhead in Surrey; and the names *Randalls* and *Knightley* came from Leatherhead.[2] In one case she relied not on fact but on previous fiction; the resemblance of Pemberley and Everingham[3] to Miss Burney's Pemberton and Everington[4] can hardly be an accident. It should seem that her creative imagination worked most freely within a framework fixed for her by small points of contact with reality.

Once she felt herself at home, her fancy would soon be busy fitting and arranging every detail. Her attentive readers quickly get the impression that she could have told much more than she did; that the lie of the country, the arrangement of the houses, the features and the dress of the people, were all envisaged. There is more than mere pleasantry in her description of Mrs. Bingley's person and costume at the exhibition—'Mrs. Bingley's

---

[1] See p. 131.
　In *Mansfield Park*.

[2] See p. 85.
[4] In *Cecilia* and *Camilla*.

is exactly herself . . . there never was a greater
likeness. She is dressed in a white gown, with
green ornaments, which convinces me of what I had
always supposed, that green was a favourite colour
with her.'[1] Family tradition records that she knew
more than she chose to make public; and some additional information has been handed down.[2] She
also recognized the limitations of her knowledge.
When she visited two exhibitions of portraits, she
had hopes of Mrs. Darcy as well as of Mrs. Bingley,
but was 'disappointed, for there was nothing like
Mrs. D. at either. I can only imagine that Mr. D.
prizes any Picture of her too much to like it should
be exposed to the public eye. I can imagine he
would have that sort of feeling—that mixture of
Love, Pride and Delicacy.' This is conjecture; but
once she cannot guess. Her niece Fanny had written
her a letter as from Elizabeth to Georgiana Darcy,

[1] Letter 80.
[2] 'In this traditionary way we learned that Miss Steele never
succeeded in catching the Doctor; that Kitty Bennet was satis-
factorily married to a clergyman near Pemberley, while Mary
obtained nothing higher than one of her uncle Philip's clerks, and
was content to be considered a star in the society of Meriton;
that the "considerable sum" given by Mrs. Norris to William
Price was one pound; that Mr. Woodhouse survived his
daughter's marriage and kept her and Mr. Knightley from
settling at Donwell, about two years; and that the letters placed
by Frank Churchill before Jane Fairfax, which she swept away
unread, contained the word "pardon".' *Memoir*, ch. 10.

announcing her engagement. 'I am very much obliged to Fanny for her letter; it made me laugh heartily; but I cannot pretend to answer it. Even had I more time, I should not feel at all sure of the sort of letter that Miss D. would write.' She knew Darcy's sister sufficiently well for her purpose, but had not studied her enough for this.

These are slight and fugitive indications; but we must make the most of them, for we are unlikely to find any better. Our author had no intention of admitting anyone to the secrets of her workshop. She polished and polished, till the finished surface of her fiction has a brilliance which delights her admirers,[1] but also an apparent hardness which has concealed from many readers the flow of imagination which lies beneath it. Because Jane Austen is content to give us the setting of her stories in brief and general terms, and leaves even her heroines' beauty[2] mainly to the imagination of those who have the wit and fancy to imagine it, it is supposed that she was ignorant or indifferent. That she gives such an impression may be her fault, or it may be ours; that is a question which will continue to divide

---

[1] 'There's a finishing off in some of her scenes that is really quite above every one else.' Scott's Journal, 14 March 1826.

[2] The dangerous alliance with the illustrator had not yet been formed. The earliest pictorial embellishments of her novels are the French frontispieces to *La Famille Elliot* (1821).

the world. But it is a consequence of her economy, not of her poverty. She dreaded being prolix or tedious; 'Heaven forbid that I should ever offer encouragement to Explanations';[1] and she relied on the reader's discernment.

> I do not write for such dull elves
> As have not a great deal of ingenuity themselves.[2]

Like many writers of fiction, Jane Austen seems to have been often dependent on the real world for a stimulus to set her fancy in motion. Patient scrutiny has discovered many points of contact between her writing and her observation or her reading; and some of them cannot be accidental. One of her early fragments[3] is clearly based on the experience of her father's sister. Her sailors owe a good deal to her own sailor brothers.[4] The origin of Fanny Price's amber cross is unmistakable.[5] The identifications made by modern critics are based,

[1] Letter 20.   [2] Letter 76. *Marmion* vi. 38:
        I do not write to that dull elf
        Who cannot image to himself. . . .
[3] See p. 41.
[4] Sir Francis Austen, accused by a correspondent of being Captain Wentworth, deprecated the compliment, but added 'I rather think parts of Captain Harville's character were drawn from myself; at least the description of his domestic habits, tastes and occupations have a considerable resemblance to mine.' Sir Francis distinguishes very properly. See J. H. Hubback in *Cornhill Magazine*, July 1928.
[5] See p. 85.

often flimsily, on definite coincidences or similari-
ties. But the assumption that her characters had
real prototypes goes back to her own time, and was
then a tribute, though a clumsy one, to her veri-
similitude. A Miss Dusautoy, we learn from the
letters,[1] 'has a great idea of being Fanny Price—
she and her youngest sister together, who is named
Fanny'. In the *Opinions* on *Emma* she notes that a
Miss Herries was 'convinced that I had meant Mrs.
and Miss Bates for some acquaintance of theirs.
People whom I never heard of before.'

The author of the *Memoir*[2] rejected all such equa-
tions, justly claiming that 'such a supposition betrays
an ignorance of the high prerogative of genius'.
He declared that 'her own relatives never recognized any individual in her characters', and adds her
own testimony.

She herself, when questioned on the subject by a
friend, expressed a dread of what she called such an
'invasion of social proprieties'. She said that she thought
it quite fair to note peculiarities and weaknesses, but
that it was her desire to create, not to reproduce;
'besides', she added, 'I am too proud of my gentlemen
to admit that they were only Mr. A. or Colonel B.'

This quotation did not come from family records
or recollections, but from the reminiscences of a

[1] Letter 97.   [2] Ch. 10.

mysterious Mrs. Barrett, communicated to Austen
Leigh by a correspondent.[1] We do not know who
Mrs. Barrett was, nor the degree of her acquaintance with Jane. But she is obviously a good witness, and Austen Leigh was entitled to accept her
evidence. We are bound to do the same. If Jane
Austen had a virtue it was truthfulness.

Even if we had not her word for it, we should find
that these identifications break down under analysis.
Mr. J. H. Hubback,[2] who as a grandson of Sir
Francis, and the repository of 'traditions and correspondence of the family', wrote with some authority, drew a series of parallels between the character
and situation of Mary Crawford and those of Eliza,
Comtesse de Feuillide. Mr. Hubback suggests,
though without giving specific evidence, that Eliza
returned to Steventon as a widow in or after 1794,
that 'it was not long before theatricals were resumed',[3] that 'Henry was again Eliza's chief co-
adjutor, and the outcome was that he became her
second husband in 1797'. We know that Henry had
been intended for the Church, but gave it up. There
is a further suggestion that Eliza's 'refusal of James
Austen in her youth was on account of his being
destined for the Church, but this may be merely

[1] See p. 116.   [2] *Cornhill Magazine*, July 1928.
[3] The earlier records end in 1790. *Life* 65.

family tradition'.[1] Here we have a situation attractively similar to the situation of *Mansfield Park*; and Mr. Hubback concludes 'that there is a considerable resemblance, in certain traits of character between the real Eliza and the imaginary Mary'. Mr. Hubback's suggestions are tentative and guarded. The outlines are hardened by Miss Thomson,[2] a sympathetic and discerning critic, who calls Mary 'a portrait from the life' and is prepared (if the tradition of James's rejection be accepted) to 'go a step further and plausibly identify Edmund Bertram with James, who is said to have directed and counselled his younger sister as Edmund directed and counselled Fanny, and may have gone to her for sympathy in his rejection'. The 'identification' of Edmund with James is not supported, indeed it is flatly contradicted, by the few indications the letters afford of Jane's estimate of her eldest brother. The identification of Mary with Eliza is more plausible, though Eliza was not the only brilliant and vivacious young woman of Jane's acquaintance. Mary's wit may well owe something to Eliza's. But a portrait is not a portrait unless it can be recognized by those

---

[1] Eliza married in 1781, when James was sixteen. She lost her husband in 1794, and James lost his wife in May 1795. James married again in January 1797. So the interval in which he could decently be thinking of Eliza is short.

[2] *Survey*, p. 148.

who know the original. Jane went to stay with Henry in 1814, and secured his enthusiastic commendation of *Mansfield Park*, and his help in publishing it. Was the portrait of Mary Crawford—who with all her wit and charm was a selfish, mercenary woman—recognized by Henry as a portrait of the wife to whom he was deeply attached and whom he had recently lost?

That William Price 'is' Charles Austen, anyone may believe who so chooses. But there is no sufficient ground for the belief. Any midshipman, affectionate, open-hearted, and adventurous, might have sat for the portrait of William Price.[1]

[1] 'We only suffer reality to suggest, not to dictate'. Charlotte Brontë, quoted in *T.L.S.* 17 July 1948, 400.

IX

ANONYMITY AND NOTORIETY

HENRY AUSTEN, in his *Notice* of his sister, writes with emphasis of her diffidence and her love of obscurity.

It was with extreme difficulty that her friends, whose partiality she suspected while she honoured their judgement, could prevail on her to publish her first work . . . so much did she shrink from notoriety, that no accumulation of fame could have induced her, had she lived, to affix her name to any production of her pen. In the bosom of her own family she talked of them freely, thankful for praise, open to remark, and submissive to criticism. But in public she turned away from any allusion to the character of an authoress.

It is clear from the letters that anonymity was precious to her. When she made her first essay in 1803, *Susan* was sold on her behalf by a person whose name gave no clue.[1] When in 1809 she tried to induce the publisher to act, she used an assumed name. Though her manuscripts were well known to her family and to a few intimate friends, the knowledge was carefully limited; and when she began to publish, secrecy was enjoined. She describes 'the caution observed at Steventon' as

[1] See p. 44.

'an agreeable surprise'.[1] Steventon must have been very cautious, for James Edward himself had read the first two novels before he knew that his aunt was their author.[2] When *Pride and Prejudice* was read aloud at Chawton, a neighbour was allowed to enjoy it; but a story had been told to avoid suspicion.[3]

It was Henry who gave her away. Soon after the publication of *Pride and Prejudice*, when she was in his house, it was suggested that she should meet a Miss Burdett. 'I should like to see Miss Burdett very well,[4] but that I am rather frightened by hearing that she wishes to be introduced to *me*. If I *am* a wild Beast, I cannot help it. It is not my own fault.' Suspicion soon turned to certainty. Henry went to Scotland, and met Lady Robert Kerr, who praised *Pride and Prejudice*; 'and what does he do in the warmth of his brotherly vanity and love, but immediately tell them who wrote it!'[5] The result of this and other indiscretions was that the secret was 'scarcely the shadow of a secret now'. She forgave Henry, but was more grateful to other members of the family, who had done as she wished and held their tongues.

[1] Letter 77.   [2] *Personal Aspects* 149.   [3] Letter 76.
[4] Perhaps because she was a sister-in-law of Sir James Langham of Cottesbrooke, the original of Mansfield Park; see p. 84.
[5] Letter 85.

I am trying to harden myself. After all, what a trifle it is in all its bearings, to the really important points of one's existence even in this world.

When people say that their troubles are 'after all trifles', we know that they are taking them to heart. There is no affectation in her dislike of notoriety. It did not deprive her of the consolation of laughing at herself—'I do not despair of having my picture in the Exhibition at last—all white and red, with my head on one side; or perhaps I may marry young Mr. D'arblay.'[1] But Henry recorded that when asked by a stranger to join a literary party at which Madame de Staël would be present, she declined the invitation.[2]

It should perhaps be added that a desire to conceal her sex was not a motive for anonymity. Women novelists were numerous and in repute; her natural ambition was to be classed with Miss Burney and Miss Edgeworth. *Sense and Sensibility* was in fact announced on its title-page to be 'By a Lady'.

Even in private her way of work was singularly quiet and inconspicuous. When she lost the 'dressing room' at Steventon she never again had a room of her own in which she could write. Her nephew

---

[1] Letter 90.
[2] *Biographical Notice* in Bentley's edition of the novels, 1833.

describes her writing at Chawton in a well-known passage.[1]

Most of the work must have been done in the general sitting-room, subject to all kinds of casual interruptions. She was careful that her occupation should not be suspected by servants, or visitors, or any persons beyond her own family party. She wrote upon small sheets of paper which could easily be put away, or covered with a piece of blotting paper. There was, between the front door and the offices, a swing door which creaked when it was opened; but she objected to having this little inconvenience remedied, because it gave her notice when anyone was coming. . . . In that well occupied female party there must have been many precious hours of silence during which the pen was busy at the little mahogany writing-desk, while Fanny Price, or Emma Woodhouse, or Anne Elliott was growing into beauty and interest. I have no doubt that I, and my sisters and cousins, in our visits to Chawton, frequently disturbed this mystic process, without having any idea of the mischief that we were doing; certainly we never should have guessed it by any signs of impatience or irritability in the writer.

Another account comes from Kent. Edward's third daughter, Marianne, was born in September 1801 and lived to 1896. Her recollections were quoted by the next generation:[2]

I remember that when Aunt Jane came to us at

[1] *Memoir*, ch. vi.   [2] I follow Miss Hill, ch. 18.

Godmersham she used to bring the MS. of whatever novel she was writing with her, and would shut herself up with my elder sisters in one of the bedrooms to read them aloud. I and the younger ones used to hear peals of laughter through the door, and thought it very hard that we should be shut out from what was so delightful. I also remember how Aunt Jane would sit quietly working beside the fire in the library, saying nothing for a good while, and then would suddenly burst out laughing, jump up and run across the room to a table where pens and paper were lying, write something down, and then come back to the fire and go on quietly working as before.

This charming story does not quite stand examination. Jane was at Godmersham in April 1809, when Marianne was under seven and her elders, Fanny and Lizzie, were sixteen and nine. It is possible that *Sense and Sensibility* or *Pride and Prejudice* was divulged during this visit. Jane was not at Godmersham again until September 1813, when *Mansfield Park* was ready for reading, and that was her last visit. But Marianne may well have confused Godmersham memories with Chawton memories; for Jane would be often at the Great House when the family was there. The accuracy of the library scene, at least, need not be doubted.

To have pleased her family was, I think, the sweetest reward of her labours. But she lived to be

gratified by the applause of many good judges outside the family. Her nephew, who as we shall see
was naturally misled by circumstances into thinking
his aunt a more obscure person than in fact she was,
went too far in saying that 'her talents did not introduce her to the notice of other writers, or connect
her with the literary world, or in any degree pierce
through the obscurity of her domestic retirement'.
She did not, indeed, actually meet any writers
of eminence, nor was she paraded in fashionable
drawing-rooms. But in the autumn of 1815, if she
was not 'a wild beast', she was rather near being
one. It is hardly doubtful that if Henry's prosperity
and her own health had continued, she must have
submitted to being famous.

Emma was read for Murray by William Gifford,
the editor of the *Quarterly*, who wrote to Murray[1]

Of *Emma* I have nothing but good to say. I was sure
of the writer before you mentioned her.

Gifford found 'many little omissions' in the manuscript, and offered to revise the book in proof. We
do not know if he did so; but Jane must have had
some communication with him, for he figures among
the critics who furnished 'hints' for her next novel.[2]
It is possible that he suggested to Murray the

[1] *Life* 310.
[2] *Plan of a Novel.*

choice of Scott as the *Quarterly* reviewer of *Emma*.
Murray wrote to Scott

Have you any fancy to dash off an article on 'Emma'—
it wants incident and romance or imagination—does it
not—none of the Author's other Novels have been
noticed & surely *Pride and Prejudice* merits high commendation.

Scott's reply was prompt, but without comment.

Inclosed is the article upon Emma. . . . It will be
quite unnecessary to send proofs of Emma, as Mr. Gifford will correct all obvious errors and abridge it where
necessary.[1]

Murray sent Jane a copy of the *Quarterly*.[2] In
returning it with her acknowledgements she refers
to her critic merely as 'so clever a man as the
Reviewer'. But she may have known or guessed
his identity. The author of the *Memoir*[3] thought it
'remarkable that living, as she did, far apart from
the gossip of the literary world, she should even
then have spoken so confidently of his being the
author' of *Waverley*. I am told by good judges that
it *is* remarkable that she should have treated it as a
certainty in September 1814.[4] But she was not so
remote from literary gossip as her biographer supposed.

The *Edinburgh* paid her no such compliment as

---

[1] *Letters of Scott*, ed. Grierson, iv. 167.
[2] Letter 127.   [3] Ch. 5.   [4] Letter 101.

the *Quarterly*. But she had the satisfaction of learning that 'Mr. Jeffrey was kept up three nights' by *Emma*.

She probably had some sort of introduction to Miss Edgeworth; without it she would hardly have sent her a presentation copy of *Emma*.[1] Miss Edgeworth's father was for many years a neighbour of Mr. Leigh Perrot in Berkshire.[2]

Another eminent admirer was Warren Hastings, who if not himself a man of letters was a generous patron of literature. Here there was a personal connexion; Eliza Austen was his god-daughter, and Henry corresponded with him, and visited him at Daylesford. It was after a visit there in 1813 that he sent him *Pride and Prejudice*; and Jane was 'quite delighted with what such a man writes about it. . . . You will hear the letter.'[3]

Jane Austen was never presented to the first gentleman in Europe. The long and entertaining story of her relations with him, their causes and their consequences, is of importance because the episode exercised her humour and drew from her some comments on her work. In itself it is of no great importance, otherwise than as the contemporary reputation of an author is of interest.

[1] *Life* 318.   [2] *Life* 126, 139.
[3] Letter 82. Hastings's letter has not survived.

It appears that Henry Austen, in his serious illness in the autumn of 1815, was attended by one of the Regent's physicians, who took the opportunity to inform his patient's sister that the Prince was an admirer of her novels 'and kept a set of them in every one of his residences'. He had thought it right to tell H.R.H. that Miss Austen was in town. The sequel to this was that the Regent's librarian waited on her, showed her over Carlton House, and intimated that a dedication would be acceptable. Jane afterwards inquired if it were incumbent on her to dedicate *Emma*. Mr. Clarke replied that it was not incumbent, but was permitted; and that settled the matter.

That she had no illusions about the Regent's character might have been guessed,[1] and is now known in a letter in which she declares for the Princess of Wales; 'Poor woman, I shall support her as long as I can, because she *is* a Woman, and because I hate her Husband.'[2] But her opinion of his morals would not affect Jane's reception of a compliment which the Regent was competent to pay, and which would be regarded as an impersonal distinction.

---

[1] It is implied in the reference to the christening of the Marquis of Granby in Letter 97; see my Index s.v. *Granby*.

[2] Unpublished letter of 16 Feb. 1813; see p. 167.

Mr. Clarke himself was a simple eccentric, without humour. He sent Jane his *Sermons*, and his edition of Falconer's *Shipwreck*, and promised her his book on James the Second. He seriously hoped to persuade her to write an 'historical romance, illustrative of the history of the august House of Coburg', or to depict a literary clergyman, resembling himself in history and character, 'no man's enemy but his own', in a work which should also advocate the abolition of tithes. These advances drew characteristic replies.

Mr. Clarke was by profession a courtier, and perhaps by nature something of a snob. His assurances that his protégée's praises had 'long been sounded as they ought to be' at Lord Egremont's at Petworth, and that 'many of the nobility' staying at the Pavilion had paid her 'the just tribute of their praise', are not worth much. But there is no reason to doubt that the Regent himself 'had read and admired all your publications' and had made it the fashion to praise them.

There is no evidence that Jane ever learned of the proof of her growing reputation given by the publication in 1815 of *Raison et Sensibilité* and in 1816 of *Le Parc de Mansfield* and *La Nouvelle Emma*. These translations were no doubt unauthorized, and may not have been known in England.

X

BIOGRAPHY AND CRITICISM

JANE AUSTEN's dislike of publicity was on the whole well supported by her family and their descendants. The pretence of anonymity had been given up immediately after her death; but for half a century there was no publication of her letters or literary fragments, or of more than the barest outline of her life. When her favourite nephew, already in his seventies, began to think that he ought to lift the veil, he consulted his sister, his half-sister, and some of his cousins. Their letters, which have survived, show the family attitude to what one member of it, Caroline Austen, called 'the vexed question between the Austens and the Public'. On the whole there was unanimity that something should be said —though one of the cousins would show letters in her possession only 'on condition of your not publishing any'. But 'it must be a difficult task to dig up the materials, so carefully have they been buried out of sight by the past generation'. And when they were dug up, which of them were fit for use?

All James Austen's three children had letters from their aunt to themselves, and of these the *Memoir* makes use. But though they revealed the beloved aunt, these letters did not tell very much of her life. Caroline 'expected little from letters'. Anna, though she knew that at Cassandra's death 'several scraps of her Sister's composition' were marked to be given to different relations, had no idea of letters surviving. 'The occasional correspondence between the Sisters when apart from each other would as a matter of course be destroyed by the Survivor. I can fancy what the indignation of Aunt Cassa would have been at the mere idea of its being read and commented upon by any of us, nephews and nieces, little or great—and indeed I think myself she was right, in that as in most other things.'

Inquiry showed that the burial had been less careful than this. The author was able to collect and print a number of Jane's letters to her sister. It was known that more existed; but their number and nature could not be discovered. Fanny Knight, Jane's favourite niece, now Lady Knatchbull of Provender, had a collection; but neither her sister nor her daughter could find them; and Lady Knatchbull having lost her memory could not be applied to on such a matter. *Lady Susan* she was asked for, and would have lent, but it was mislaid.[1]

Caroline Austen's opinion of the family letters

[1] It was printed from a copy, see p. 163.

she had seen is stated in her memorandum of 1867.[1] She did not think they would be acceptable to the public: 'They must have been very interesting to those who received them, but they detailed chiefly home and family events and she seldom committed herself even to any opinion, so that to strangers there could be no transcript of her mind.' The letters to Cassandra she seems not to have seen, but she knew what had become of them. 'Her letters to Aunt Cassandra were, I daresay,[2] open and confidential. My Aunt looked them over and burnt the greater part as she told me three or four years before her own death. She left or gave some as legacies to the nieces, but of those that I have seen several had portions cut out.'[3] It has been stated that Cassandra's motive was the fear that the letters might be published after her death, but this may be a mere inference. Whatever her reasons, she was remarkably successful in suppressing anything of peculiar intimacy. There is, for example, no allusion to their brother George, or to the Bigg-Wither affair.[4] The very few allusions which we might have expected her to suppress, such as those

---

[1] See p. 169.

[2] That is, 'I am confident'.

[3] Several of the Brabourne letters have lost small pieces, carefully removed with scissors.

[4] See p. 61.

to her own (Cassandra's) engagement,[1] and to Mr. Blackall,[2] were perhaps overlooked.

The division of the treasures between the two favourite nieces is easily understood. Anna had had literary ambitions as a girl; Aunt Jane had read her manuscripts, and written her long delightful letters about them. It was natural that she should be given *Sanditon* and the fragment of *Persuasion*. The letters, on the other hand, would be more interesting to Fanny, since nearly all of them were written from, or to, Godmersham or its neighbourhood. The small group of letters which was given to Charles Austen, or perhaps to his daughter Cassandra, is entirely non-Kentish.

The ladies were more hopeful of literary 'scraps' than of letters. Anna offered the lines on Mrs. Lefroy's death—'but perhaps you may think them too long'; they were printed, almost in full.[3] Caroline offered nonsense verses, and thought her brother might consider 'the story, I believe in your possession, all nonsense. I don't mean Kitty's Bower, but the other—of the gentleman who wanders forth and is put in possession of a stranger's house, and married to his daughter Maria.'[4] This 'clever non-

---

[1] See p. 16.   [2] See p. 60.

[3] Two additional stanzas are published in *The Times*, 12 May 1936. The autograph was sold at Sotheby's, 3 May 1948.

[4] That is, *Evelyn*, in *Volume the Third*, see p. 162.

sense' might not be well received; but 'something must *ever* be risked'. But she was clear—and here she finds some modern sympathizers—against the publication of the more mature pieces. 'What I should deprecate is publishing any of the "betweenities" when the nonsense was passing away, and before her wonderful talent had found its proper channel. Lady Knatchbull has a whole short story they were wishing years ago to make public—but were discouraged by others—and I hope the desire has passed away.' In the event, the biographer fought shy of the juvenile effusions (except *The Mystery*) but was prevailed on to divulge the 'betweenities', and even persuaded Anna to let him make extracts from *Sanditon*. But another half-century passed before Anna's granddaughter made up her mind to publish the whole of *Sanditon*.

When Lady Knatchbull died her son examined her papers and found not only the missing autograph *Lady Susan* but also 'a square box full of letters', the contents of which he describes with affectionate particularity. Edward Knatchbull-Hugesson, first Lord Brabourne, was a man of letters as well as a politician, and well known in his day as a writer of stories for children. He was too late for *Lady Susan*; but the letters offered temptations which it would have been hard to withstand. His book has been called garrulous, and is certainly discursive; but he appreciated the letters, and treated them in the right way, as a piece of family and county history. For this he was well qualified, having an inexhaustible and infectious delight in genealogy and anecdote. His fault as an editor is that he was ignorant of the Hampshire connexion. It is clear, from the letters quoted above, that there had been little intercourse between the Godmersham Austens (Knights) and the other branches of the family. Lord Brabourne in his introduction writes of the author of the *Memoir* as of a stranger, and represents him as unaware of the existence of the letters which had been given to Fanny Knight. Austen Leigh, on his side, shows little knowledge of the life which his aunts led when they made their long visits in Kent. This mutual ignorance led to some misconception.

Handicapped as he felt himself to be by the limitations of his own knowledge, and the poverty of written materials, Jane Austen's first biographer sketched an outline which is just and satisfactory. In the forty years which followed a number of short lives and essays were published, but none of these made any important addition except Miss Hill's[1]

[1] 1901. See p. 170.

little book and Lord Brabourne's edition[1] of the *Letters*, which drew from a fresh source. It was not until 1913 that a son and grandson of James Edward Austen Leigh, with almost all the materials open to them, produced what may fairly be called a definitive life. Intensive study of the novels and fragments, and of the letters, though it has added much to criticism, has added little to the Austen Leighs' picture of Jane Austen, and I believe has taken nothing from it.

The criticism of the novels begins with family verdicts recorded in the letters,[2] and is continued in the Opinions on *Mansfield Park* and on *Emma* which the author collected and transcribed. Though these were communicated to members of the authors' family, they are not exclusively polite or affectionate. There is much of preferences—of this novel (usually, of course, *Pride and Prejudice*) or that, or of this or that character. Fanny Price moves between the extremes of 'a delightful character' and 'insipid', and Mrs. Rushworth's elopement between 'unnatural' (Jane's nephew and future biographer) and 'very natural' (his mother). One clergyman, supported by one lady, 'thought the Authoress wrong, in such times as these, to draw

---

[1] 1884; see p. 166.

[2] These are collected in my edition, Index VI.

such Clergymen as Mr. Collins and Mr. Elton';
but another clergyman and his wife were 'particularly pleased with the manner in which the Clergy
are treated'. Mr. and Mrs. Cooke were thinking
of Sir Thomas Bertram's exemplary views on the
duties of a parish priest. A Lady Gordon was perhaps the foundress of a tradition which treats Jane
Austen's world as a real world: 'You fancy yourself one of the family.' Later, Macaulay and his
sisters used the dialogue of the novels as the cur-
rency of familiar talk. Miss Isabella Herries was
'convinced that I had meant Mrs. and Miss Bates for
some acquaintance of theirs—people whom I never
heard of before'. This is perhaps the first of an
interminable series of baseless and tiresome identifications.

But Jane Austen's fame soon passed from a narrow circle into the safer keeping of men of letters.
Scott, as we saw, wrote a *Quarterly* review of
Emma. He read the novels till the well-worn condition of the Abbotsford set could be remarked,[1]
and confided to his journal his almost envious
admiration of their author's talent.[2] Coleridge
and Southey praised her truth and individuality.
Macaulay, and later Tennyson, put her 'next to
Shakespeare'; a judgement which, echoed without

---

[1] *Memoir*, p. 149.   [2] See pp. 101, 124.

qualification,[1] has done her reputation more harm than good. Miss Mitford, though she repeated, and perhaps credited, descriptions of Jane Austen, both in youth and in middle age, which were exceedingly unfavourable, was unable to visit Bath without 'the tenderest recollections of her exquisite *Persuasion*'.[2]

Charlotte Brontë's dissent from the general approval might perhaps have been assumed. It will be found in her correspondence[3] with George Henry Lewes. It is fair to say that Lewes did not go the best way to recommend his favourite novelist by prescribing her works as a sedative; Miss Brontë was to learn from her to shun melodrama and 'be more subdued'. When, in proclaiming her 'one of the greatest artists', and 'one of the writers with the nicest sense of means to an end', he insisted that she had neither poetry nor even 'sentiment', he invited the retort that, in Miss Brontë's eyes, no writer without these qualities could be great. It was the sentiment in Thackeray's large heart that converted 'corrosive poison into purifying elixir'.

[1] 'Shakespeare, however, is a sun to which Jane Austen, tho' a bright and true little world, is but an asteroid.' *Life of Tennyson*, by his son, 1897, ii. 371.

[2] 'I doubt if anyone, even Scott himself, have left such perfect impressions of character and place as Jane Austen.' *Recollections of a Literary Life*, 1852, ii. 197. For the other side of the picture see p. 120.

[3] 1848. Mrs. Gaskell's *Life*, 1857, ii, ch. 2.

It is remarkable that Trollope, who was born in
1815 and believed that Harrow and Winchester had
left him as ignorant as they received him, had at
nineteen 'already made up his mind that *Pride &
Prejudice* was the best novel in the English language'.
He rather rubbed the gilt off the gingerbread by a
later suspicion that *Ivanhoe* might be better, and
a final assurance that *Esmond* was best.   But we
may be satisfied with his 'first impressions'.

With such general, aphoristic judgements as I
have quoted the nineteenth century was for the
most part content. The Victorians read and enjoyed the novels, but did not make them a critical
touchstone; Jane Austen did not divide the world,
as Dickens and Thackeray divided it on a literary
issue. Elaborate or technical criticism of her work
begins with Andrew Bradley's essay[1] published in
1911. Even in our time good criticism has not
been plentiful; nearly all of it is in reviews or
occasional essays.

The critics have not much debated Jane Austen's
construction. It has been generally allowed that
her plots—though not always that their cata-
strophes—are artistically satisfying. Mr. Garrod
(for whose essay in denigration see below[2]) makes
his best point when he complains that the situation

[1] See p. 170.   [2] p. 171.

is, broadly, always the same: a village, containing a young woman, or two young women, to which Young Eligible arrives as a visitor; the husband-hunt ensuing. But as a rule Jane Austen's own choice of situation—'such a spot is the delight of my life; three or four families in a country village is the very thing to work on'[1]—has been accepted without demur. Criticism has rather been busy with the inhabitants of the village. Treating them as real people, it has inquired nicely into questions of coherence and probability; is Mr. Collins a caricature? Is Edmund Bertram a prig, or Fanny Price a prude? And to those who answer these questions unfavourably, a further and larger question presents itself: did his author know Edmund to be a prig? Almost certainly not; she intended us to like him, and to approve him as the object of Fanny's passion.[2] This raises the question of her 'limitations'; how far they were self-imposed, how far due to lack of experience or lack of intuition; and if self-imposed, then how far justified; for ignorance, though in itself a good reason for narrowing the canvas, might be due to culpable negligence.

It is common ground that her knowledge of men

[1] Letter 100.
[2] I ignore those critics—they exist—who assert that J. A. knew nothing about passion.

was limited not only by the barrier of sex but also by environment; she had not the opportunities of a George Eliot. But some go farther. Walter Raleigh, whom I quoted earlier, conceding that 'she knows a lot', that her 'young women are incomparable', and willing to believe 'that she knows what she does not know', found no reality, or none of the right kind, in her young men. 'There is no indication that they can *do* anything. . . . They would be black-balled in any club.'[1] If this were true it would be a grave defect. But Raleigh had to admit that 'it deludes you while you read'. That is asking too much of credulity; delusions on that scale do not endure. Most judges are content to agree with the common reader that Jane Austen knows her young men well enough for her purpose; in relation, that is, to the young women on whom the searchlight of her imaginative sympathy is focused. The subject of her art is not individuals but their interaction. We are entitled to be content with her selection from life, to take it on her own terms, if we can rest satisfied that it is not misleading.

The best critics of Jane Austen have been those who have read and reread her books, finding in them an inexhaustible source of interest and delight. Mere accuracy and artistry cannot yield such in-

[1] *Letters*, 23 Oct. 1917. See p. 118.

terest; and these critics have seen that Jane Austen is larger than her theme. It is, in Scott's phrase, 'the truth of the description and the sentiment' that holds us. Walter Raleigh expressed the same conviction more fully and precisely when he wrote that 'the world of pathos and passion is present in her work by implication'.[1] The sentiment would not be true if it were not catholic. The highly entertaining comic figure of Miss Bates is also substantial and beautiful, because her author knew and loved her absurd old maid, for her virtues and her poverty as well as for her folly. Her satire is merciless; it admits no extenuation; but it is not misanthropy.

All the hostile criticism of Jane Austen amounts to little more than this, that she was not a poet. In that respect—and in that alone?—she is inferior to Dickens, to Emily Brontë, to Hardy. Now the highest expression, in literature, of our spiritual and emotional nature is poetry. But our intellectual and practical activities are best guided, disciplined, and fortified by prose. This troubled world, then, groping for guidance but impatient of discipline, has room for such a writer as Jane Austen. Her works give a great deal of harmless pleasure; but they do much more than that; they 'instruct by

[1] *The English Novel*, 1894, 263.

pleasing', which is what she meant they should do. To the thoughtful reader they can give also what Boswell got from the *Rambler*, 'Bark and steel for the mind'.[1]

[1] That is, quinine and iron.

ADDENDUM

A reprint allows me to add a reference to Mr. Edwin Mair's admirable article in the *New York Times Book Review*, 28 August 1949.

XI

JANE AUSTEN AND HER PUBLISHERS

THE commercial history of the novels can be made out in some detail[1] from the letters and other evidence. She describes one of her publishers —Mr. John Murray himself—as 'a rogue of course', and herself as a mercenary author. These denunciations will not be taken very seriously except by those critics who choose to believe her sincere when she confesses a vice, and hypocritical when she assumes a virtue.

Her first publisher, Thomas Egerton of the Military Library in Whitehall, published two editions of *Sense and Sensibility* and one of *Mansfield Park* at the author's expense, three editions of *Pride and Prejudice* at his own. He bought *Pride and Prejudice* outright for £110.[2] Jane knew she was making a bad bargain. She had asked for £150, a very modest demand, since she had made £140 by a small edition of *Sense and Sensibility*.[3] Characteristically she makes excuses for Egerton; 'we could not both be pleased, and I am not at all surprised

---

[1] See Keynes, *Bibliography*, and my article in *London Mercury*, Aug. 1930.　　　　　[2] Letter 74. 1.
[3] Letter 81.

that he should not chuse to hazard so much'. Egerton must have made a handsome profit. There is no reason to suppose that he consulted or even informed her about the second edition. Her ignorance would explain her otherwise surprising failure to correct bad misprints which she had herself detected.[1] She made careful changes in the second editions of *Sense and Sensibility* and *Mansfield Park*.[2]

She never calls Egerton a rogue, and probably she would have stuck to him if he had been reasonably efficient. But he seems to have been unaccountably hesitant on the question of a second edition of *Mansfield Park*;[3] perhaps he hoped to buy it cheaply. For whatever reason, she transferred her favours to Mr. Murray, and in her brief season of literary fame basked in the sunshine of compliment and attention from Albemarle Street.

Murray offered £450 for the copyrights of *Sense and Sensibility*, *Mansfield Park*, and *Emma*. Henry

[1] Letter 77. The reference (Letter 91, 6 Nov. 1813) to a copy of 'my second edition' doubtless refers to *S. and S.* not, as has been assumed, to *P. and P.*

[2] There is no such excuse for her failure to correct equally bad misprints in *M. P.* But it was in December 1815 (Letter 121) that she sent Murray a copy, 'as ready for a second edition, I believe, as I can make it'. Preoccupation with *Emma*, and with her brother's serious illness and more serious business troubles, may explain this inadvertence.

[3] Letters 103, 106.

Austen in reply pointed out that his sister had made more out of 'one very moderate edition of *Mansfield Park* (you yourself expressed astonishment that so small an edition of such a work should have been sent into the world) and a still smaller one of *Sense and Sensibility*'.[1] The offer was not accepted, and Murray published the first edition of *Emma* and the second of *Mansfield Park* on profit-sharing terms.

Towards the end of her life Jane made a memorandum of the 'Profits of my Novels, over and above the £600 in the Navy Fives'.[2] The choice of investment must have enhanced the author's pride of performance. The additional figures are some £39 'first profits of *Emma*' and £45 from Egerton on the two older books. By the end of 1818 Murray owed Cassandra, as her legatee, £459 for *Northanger Abbey and Persuasion*.

The records in Albemarle Street show that 2,000 copies were printed of *Emma*. From this and the indications quoted above, together with the relative frequency of the surviving copies, the numbers

[1] *Life* 310.

[2] Morgan Library. Facsimile in *Plan of a Novel*. The profit on the first edition of *S. and S.* was £140; this, by rule of three, would give a total of £560 for *S. and S.* and *M. P.*, which with £110 for *P. and P.* makes £670. At the date of the memorandum J. A. had cleared £645 from these three books, and the second edition of *M. P.* was still recent.

printed of the first editions have been estimated as follows: *S. & S.*, 750 or 1,000; *P. & P.*, 1,250 or 1,500; *M. P.*, 1,250 or 1,500; *Emma*, 2,000; *N. A. and P.*, 2,500. The total sales of the novels, in the editions printed during, or just after, the author's death, would be approximately: *S. & S.*, 2,000; *P. & P.*, 4,000; *M. P.*, 3,000; *Emma*, 2,000; *N. A. and P.*, 2,500.

No more was done for fifteen years, and *Emma* in particular must have suffered from the lack of copies. In 1832 Bentley was anxious to include the novels in his series. He had a conversation with Henry Austen 'respecting any biographical relics of the Author', and received from him a letter written on behalf of Cassandra and himself as joint proprietors of the copyrights. This letter referred him to Egerton's executors for *Pride and Prejudice*, and accepted his offer of £250 for the five other books.

The later history is sketched in Chapter XII.

XII

AUTHORITIES

BIBLIOGRAPHY

Jane Austen: A Bibliography. By Geoffrey Keynes. 1929. This work surveys with affectionate 'particularity', the original editions, early American editions and French translations, collected editions and separate reprints, letters, miscellaneous writings, biography, and criticism in books and periodicals.

The article in the *Cambridge Bibliography of English Literature*, 1940, is described as 'Revised by R. W. Chapman'. This is inaccurate. I had, in fact, in pursuance of my instructions, made a careful selection, ignoring the numerous books and articles that I thought not worth reading, and including a few important reviews. When I was told that the plan of the work had been altered to include *all* books and articles (*except* reviews), I replied in effect 'Do what you think right, but don't say I did it'.

THE NOVELS

SENSE AND SENSIBILITY: A NOVEL. In Three Volumes. By a Lady. Vol. I (etc.). London: Printed for the

Author, by C. Roworth, Bell-Yard, Temple-bar, and Published by T. Egerton, Whitehall. 1811. 15s. in boards.

Second edition (corrected) 1813.

PRIDE AND PREJUDICE: A NOVEL. In Three Volumes. By the Author of 'Sense and Sensibility'. Vol. I (etc.). London: Printed for T. Egerton, Military Library, Whitehall. 1813. 18s. in boards.

Second edition (not revised by the author) 1813. Third edition (in two volumes) 1817.

MANSFIELD PARK: A NOVEL. In Three Volumes. By the Author of 'Sense and Sensibility' and 'Pride and Prejudice'. Vol. I (etc.). London: Printed for T. Egerton, Military Library, Whitehall. 1814. 18s. in boards.

Second edition (corrected) published by John Murray 1816.

EMMA: A NOVEL. In Three Volumes. By the Author of 'Pride and Prejudice', &c. &c. Vol. I (etc.). London: Printed for John Murray. 1816. 21s. in boards.

NORTHANGER ABBEY: AND PERSUASION. By the Author of 'Pride and Prejudice', 'Mansfield Park', &c. With a Biographical Notice of the Author. In Four Volumes. Vol. I (etc.). London. John Murray, Albemarle-Street. 1818. 24s. in boards.

For the cancelled chapter see below, p. 163; for the Biographical Notice, p. 168.

After 1818 there was no new edition of any of the novels until Bentley in 1833 produced his collected edition in five volumes, issued both as a collection and as part of his larger series of 'standard novels'.[1] This edition was reprinted in 1866 and 1869, and again in 1878–9, with the addition of a sixth volume containing the *Memoir*, &c., and styled *Lady Susan* (see p. 162), and in 1882. This edition was the form in which Jane Austen was best known to Victorian readers. There were, however, five other separate editions[2] of *Pride and Prejudice* between 1844 and 1860, by which date all the copyrights had lapsed, and three or four of the other novels.[3] After 1870 editions became fairly numerous, *Pride and Prejudice* remaining the favourite. None the less, the appearance in 1892 of Dent's edition in ten volumes, with new illustrations (replacing Bentley's frontispieces, which were pre-Victorian), marked a revival which has gone on until our own time. Jane Austen and (perhaps!)

[1] In view of her established reputation, and the modest size of the editions, the interval (fifteen years at the shortest) may seem surprising. But the public for such fiction was still not very large, and there were no cheap editions. The novels must have circulated briskly from the libraries and in the book-clubs which then flourished throughout the country.

[2] I rely on Keynes's *Bibliography*.

[3] A few years before the publication of the *Memoir*, a verger in Winchester Cathedral was wondering 'whether there was anything particular about that lady'; so many people inquired for her grave. The story nicely illustrates the diffusion of her fame.

Sir Walter Scott are the only pre-Victorian novelists who can now be called widely or generally popular.[1]

I refer to the novels by Volume and Chapter[2] or by the pages of my own edition (Oxford 1923; reprinted with some corrections 1926 and again 1933 and later).

JUVENILIA

Jane Austen preserved in three quarto note-books, styled 'Volume the First', &c., a collection of her juvenile performances, some of which are dated, or are fixed as earlier than a known date by the description of the persons to whom they are dedicated; the dates range from June 1790 to June 1793, when the author was not yet eighteen. The three volumes were preserved by Cassandra Austen, who was doubtless without fear of their publication, and (presumably at her death) passed (1) to Charles Austen ('I think I recollect that a few of the trifles in this Vol. were written expressly for his amusement', is Cassandra's note); (2) to Sir Francis

[1] I have it on good authority that J. A. is now the only nineteenth-century prose writer with whom the rising genera-tion (including aspirants to honours in English Literature) can be assumed familiar.

[2] The retention of the original numeration has its incon-veniences, since most modern reprints have the chapters num-bered throughout; but it is important. Novels were written in two, three, &c., volumes; the division was not left to the printer. A volume may have its own symmetry and its own climax.

Austen; (3) to James Edward Austen Leigh. 'Volume I' was long lost, and known only by a short extract[1] from it printed in the *Memoir*. In 1933 it was acquired by the Friends of the Bodleian and printed at Oxford (ed. R. W. C.). 'Volume II' was published in 1922, as 'Love and Freindship', by authority of Mrs. Sanders, Sir Francis's granddaughter. 'Volume III' remains unpublished.

For a list of the titles of the various pieces see *Volume the First* (1933), p. 139.

OTHER POSTHUMOUS WORKS

The author of the *Memoir* of 1870, yielding to pressure from correspondents, added to his second edition (1871) the short sketch which he called *Lady Susan*, the fragment which he called *The Watsons*, the cancelled chapter of *Persuasion*, and extracts from the 'Last Work' now known as *Sanditon*. This had the consequence, not intended by the biographer, that his book was lettered 'Lady Susan &c.', and under that style took and maintained its place as one volume in Bentley's collected edition of the novels. All four pieces have been printed or reprinted at Oxford from the autographs (ed. R. W. C.: *Sanditon* 1925, *Lady Susan* 1928,

---

[1] 'The Mystery.' *Life* 53–7. Duplicates of 'Volume I', or of parts of it, are among the Austen Leigh family papers.

Two Chapters of Persuasion 1926, *The Watsons* 1927).

Lady Susan. The autograph (on paper with a watermark of 1805) was given or bequeathed by Cassandra Austen to her niece Fanny Knight. The author of the *Memoir* had the leave of the owner (then Lady Knatchbull) to print it, but he used not the autograph, which could not then be found, but a not very accurate copy.[1] The original became the property of the Earl of Rosebery, and was sold at Sotheby's on 27 June 1933 for £2,100.

The Watsons was printed by the author of the *Memoir* from the autograph belonging to his sister (? Anna Lefroy as Brabourne says, or Caroline Austen as seems more likely), which is on paper bearing a watermark of 1803. The first six leaves of the manuscript were sold by the late William Austen Leigh at a Red Cross sale in 1918, and are now in the Pierpont Morgan Library. The bulk of the manuscript is the property of Mr. Austen Leigh's legatees.

Persuasion. This manuscript—the only surviving manuscript of any part of the six novels—was dated by Jane Austen, at various points, 'July 8'; 'Finis. July 16. 1816'; 'Finis. July 18. 1816'. It comprises chapters 10 and 11, so numbered, of the second

[1] Brabourne i. ix.

volume. J. A. as is well known was dissatisfied with chapter 10; and in recasting she substituted for it two new chapters, 10 and 11. The original 11 thus became 12; but it was revised and rewritten, and accordingly the concluding chapter of *Persuasion*, as well as a cancelled chapter, has survived in manuscript. The Oxford edition of 1926 contains, in some copies, a facsimile of the whole. The manuscript was given to Anna Lefroy, and was acquired by the British Museum from her granddaughter, the late Miss Isabel Lefroy.

Sanditon. The manuscript of the work traditionally so named was dated by J. A., at various points, 'Jan: 27. 1817', 'March 1st', 'March 18'. Only brief extracts from it were given in the *Memoir*, and the Oxford edition of 1925 is regarded as the first. The manuscript belonged to Anna Lefroy, and was given by Miss Lefroy to King's College, Cambridge, of which college her kinsman Augustus Austen Leigh was Provost.

The *Memoir* (1871) contained also a satirical piece *Plan of a Novel according to Hints from Various Quarters*. An Oxford edition (1926) gives, with facsimiles, the *Plan*, the correspondence with the Prince Regent's librarian which occasioned it, and *Opinions* on *Mansfield Park* and on *Emma* collected and written down by J. A. These manuscripts were owned by descendants of Charles Austen,[1] from whom they were acquired by the British Museum (the *Opinions*) and the Morgan Library (the *Plan* and correspondence).

These are Jane Austen's *opuscula*. It remains to mention occasional verses of her composition quoted in the *Memoir*, by Lord Brabourne, or in the *Life* (1913), and a volume of family *Charades* (three of them by J. A.) published in 1895. Notes by J. A. in her copy of Goldsmith's *History of England* (1771) are quoted in *Personal Aspects* (see below).

In the collection preserved in Charles Austen's family was a manuscript containing three 'evening prayers' for domestic use. The manuscript is partly in J. A.'s hand, and is endorsed by Charles 'Prayers composed by my ever-dear sister Jane'. It has been printed (San Francisco, 1940).

LETTERS

Of Jane Austen's surviving letters the greater number are to her sister Cassandra. There are also letters to her brothers Francis and Charles, to her nephew James Edward Austen (Leigh), her nieces Anna Austen (Lefroy), Caroline Austen, and Fanny

[1] For a fuller account of this collection see my edition of the *Memoir*, p. xi, or *The Times Literary Supplement*, 14 Jan. 1926.

Knight; with a few more to friends, acquaintances, and publishers.

Until 1932 these letters were accessible in the following books:

The *Memoir* 1870–1. The author had access to all the family letters which had survived, except those owned by Lady Knatchbull (Fanny Knight), the state of whose health prevented any application to her. The letters which were inherited by the Austen Leigh family are on deposit in the British Museum, the letters to Anna were given to St. John's College, Oxford, by Miss Isabel Lefroy in 1938.

Letters of Jane Austen edited by Edward, Lord Brabourne. 1884. These were letters from J. A. to Cassandra, given by the latter to Fanny Knight, with five from J. A. to Fanny Knight herself and two from C. E. A. to Fanny after J. A.'s death. Thus *Memoir* and *Letters* are complementary and do not overlap, except that Lord Brabourne added to his own collection a few letters to Anna Lefroy furnished by one of her daughters.

Jane Austen's Sailor Brothers by J. H. and E. C. Hubback, 1906, first made known the letters to Francis Austen. These belonged to his grandson Captain Ernest Austen, R.N., who afterwards gave them to the British Museum.

The authoritative *Life and Letters of Jane Austen* by William and Richard A. Austen Leigh, son and grandson of the first biographer (1913; 2nd ed. 1913; now unhappily out of print), used all the letters previously known, and added others. But the *Life and Letters* does not purport to be a complete edition of the letters, though it quotes almost all of them.

As editions of the letters, therefore, though not otherwise, all these works were superseded in 1932 by my own *Jane Austen's Letters to her Sister Cassandra and Others* (Oxford, two volumes), which for the first time gave the full text of all known letters or fragments of letters. This edition depends for the most part on the originals, or reliable copies of the originals, and not on printed sources. For some thirty of the Brabourne letters I had to print the text of 1884, being unable to trace the originals. A few of them have come to light since, but these reveal no very serious imperfections in Lord Brabourne's print.

My edition gives the ownership of all letters traced up to 1932, and the history of any previous publication. A new letter to Martha Lloyd (16 Feb. 1813; 78.1 in my numeration) was sold at Sotheby's 1 August 1933; the courtesy of the vendor enabled me to secure a copy.

BIOGRAPHY, FAMILY HISTORY, CRITICISM

The *Biographical Notice of the Author* by Henry Austen, prefixed to the posthumous edition of *Northanger Abbey and Persuasion*, and slightly expanded as an introduction to Bentley's collected edition of 1833, is very brief and general. Though it reveals the author's name, and extols her genius and virtues, it gives only a handful of facts.

Apart from this contemporary tribute, the only published account of Jane Austen by one who knew her is the *Memoir* mentioned above, published in 1870 by her nephew James Edward Austen Leigh. Lord Brabourne's *Letters* is valuable for its full account of J. A.'s life in Kent, of which the *Memoir* knows little. The *Life* was based on an exhaustive knowledge not only of published sources but also of many unpublished family manuscripts. The most important of these were placed at my disposal in editing the Letters.

Correspondence on the *Memoir*: J. E. A. L. kept in a volume, now owned by Mr. Richard Austen Leigh, letters from his sister, his half-sister, and others, written in or about 1869, giving him information or advice. These contain a good deal of information not published in the *Memoir*.

Reminiscences by Caroline Austen, J. A.'s niece,

owned by Mr. E. C. Austen Leigh, have the value
of contemporary evidence, since they were based
on 'the entries in my Mother's well-kept pocket-
book'. Her memorandum on life at Chawton Cottage, quoted in *Personal Aspects* (see below), and
other notes by her were written from memory in
or about 1867.

A manuscript note-book by Anna Lefroy, in the
possession of the late Miss Isabel Lefroy, contains
much interesting family history. It is supplemented
by a second note-book by Anna's daughter Mrs.
Bellas. Mrs. Bellas's copy of the 1884 *Letters*,
owned by Mrs. Raymond Hartz, has some valuable
notes.

A number of volumes, published or privately
printed, contain local information and family history. The author of the *Memoir* himself printed in
1865 *Recollections of the Early Days of the Vine Hunt
by a Sexagenarian*. His own life by his daughter
Mary Augusta was privately printed in 1911. This
Miss Austen Leigh in 1920 published *Personal
Aspects of Jane Austen*, in which she supplemented
the *Life* by her kinsmen with further quotation of
family papers.

Occasional details are furnished by *Passages from
the Diary of Mrs. Philip Lybbe Powys of Hard-
wick*, edited by Mrs. Climenson in 1899 (for the

connexion see p. 5), by the unpublished Powlett Correspondence (see my *Letters* i, p. xxxvii), and by *Chawton Manor and its Owners* by William Austen Leigh and Montagu George Knight, 1911. Miss Constance Hill in 1901 published *Jane Austen, Her Homes and Her Friends*, a pleasing account of the family and its environment derived from family papers and traditions.

MODERN CRITICISM

For the opinions of Scott, Coleridge, Southey, and of Macaulay, Trollope, Charlotte Brontë, Tennyson, and other Victorians, see the *Memoir*, or above, Chapter X.

A. C. Bradley's essay in *Essays and Studies by Members of the English Association*, vol. ii (1911), has been much read and quoted, and has been regarded as a fresh starting-point. Bradley was whole-hearted in his admiration, but made no extravagant claims.

Mr. E. M. Forster gave to his review of the Oxford edition of the novels (*Nation*, 5 Jan. 1924) the engaging title 'Jane, how shall we ever recollect?' (that is, 'half the dishes for grandmamma': from Miss Bates's great speech on entering the supper-room at the Crown).[1] Mr. Forster's own

---

[1] In *Abinger Harvest*, 1936, this and other reviews are reprinted with more ordinary labels.

fiction resembles Jane Austen's in its affectionate concern for domestic interiors; and on that plane his criticism is subtle and sympathetic. In his review of *Sanditon* (*Nation*, 21 March 1925) he found in the fragment not only evidence of fatigue but also a change of tone which might have led her to a new criticism of life. For his depreciation of the Letters see above, p. 106.

Virginia Woolf's essay on Jane Austen in her collection *The Common Reader* (1925) comprehends, in its concluding paragraphs, her review of the novels, 'Jane Austen at Sixty' (*Nation*, 15 Dec. 1923). Mrs. Woolf on Jane Austen is, as might be expected, good criticism as well as good Woolf: characteristic flash-lighting. She apprehends her greatness, 'her exquisite discrimination of human values'; but also that she is 'of all great writers the most difficult to catch in the act of greatness'. Like Mr. Forster, Mrs. Woolf is struck by the transition in the last works; she finds in *Persuasion* a peculiar beauty as well as a 'peculiar dullness', and speculates on the quality of the novels she did not live to write: 'she would have been the forerunner of Henry James[1] and of Proust'.

Mr. H. W. Garrod's 'Jane Austen: a Depreciation', published in the *Transactions of the Royal*

[1] This is also in Kipling's *The Janeites*, 1924. See p. 204.

Society of Literature (*Essays by Divers Hands*, vol. viii, 1928), was originally written 'for a pleasant occasion', and almost purports to be an essay in misrepresentation. Like Charlotte Brontë, Mr. Garrod had had the novels forced upon him by an indiscreet admirer. But he shrewdly observes of his own performance that 'the malice is the best part of it'. His sophistry is weighted and sharpened by a genuine distaste for his subject. My own attempt at refutation—made, perhaps, with some excess of zeal—may be read in the transactions of the same society (*Essays*, vol. x, 1931).

Miss Elizabeth Bowen in 1936 contributed to *The English Novelists* (edited by Derek Verschoyle) a short essay on Jane Austen which is full of striking, if often disputable, judgements.

Many men of letters have written introductions to reprints of one or more of the novels. Some of them have been illustrative, like E. V. Lucas's discussion of the original of Highbury, or Mr. Michael Sadleir's of the 'horrid' novels celebrated in *Northanger Abbey*; others more critical. George Saintsbury accelerated the growth of Jane Austen's popularity by his introduction to an edition of *Pride and Prejudice* published by G. Allen 1894, and embellished with pictures by Hugh Thomson, which were much admired and are, I hope, now forgotten.

John Cann Bailey wrote introductions to all the novels, and collected them in a volume (1931). His criticism was described by an eminent reviewer as 'lucidly discriminating' and 'pleasantly fond'. I have confessed that I find it somewhat pontifical.

There is good analysis in the introductions to *Sense-and Sensibility* (Lord David Cecil) and *Mansfield Park* (Miss Mary Lascelles) in the World's Classics (1931 and 1929).

Miss C. Linklater Thomson's *Jane Austen a Survey*, 1929, is a full, well-documented, and sympathetic account of the writer and her works.

Lord David Cecil's Leslie Stephen Lecture[1] (Cambridge 1935) is, I believe, the only brief account of Jane Austen as an artist and a moralist that is completely satisfactory. If he anywhere fails to reach the root of the matter, it is in his too summary dealing with Jane Austen's detractors. Marcus Aurelius described the jurymen who condemned Socrates as 'lice'. Lord David writes, with almost equal terseness, 'there are those who do not like sunshine or unselfishness'. He is right in his perception that the novels are, in fact, radiant with the sunshine of unselfishness. But I think Jane Austen

[1] An appropriate occasion, for the short life in the *D.N.B.* was by the great editor himself.

would have been more tolerant of good people to whom that perception was denied.

Miss Mary Lascelles's *Jane Austen and her Art* (1939, and so not entered in the *Cambridge Bibliography of English Literature*) is an intensive study of artistic technique. She is perhaps a critic's critic, and moves in a rare atmosphere. She was better fitted for her ambitious enterprise than most of us; for she shares, with her sex, many of Jane Austen's opinions and tastes, and her love of nice distinctions and fine proprieties: what Robert Bridges called 'keeping'.

Miss Elizabeth Jenkins's book is written with a humility rare in literary critics; so much so that a careless reader might miss some very shrewd intuitions. This is a singularly honest book, the spontaneous effusion of real affection.[1]

Of my own contribution I mention an article on 'Jane Austen's Methods' (*The Times Literary Supplement*, 9 Feb. 1922); my introduction to the *Letters*, in which I claim to have placed those documents in true perspective; and an article in the forthcoming new edition of Chambers's *Encyclopaedia*.

[1] My comment is on the first edition, 1938; a revised edition was published in 1948.

CHRONOLOGY[1]

1764   26 Apr. George Austen (born 1731) m. Cassandra
       Leigh.

1765   13 Feb. James A. born.

1766   26 Aug. George A. born.

1768   7 Oct. Edward Austen (Knight 1812) born.

1771   8 June. Henry Thomas A. baptized.

1773   9 Jan. Cassandra Elizabeth A. born.

1774   23 Apr. Francis William A. born.

1775   16 Dec. Jane A. born.

1779   23 June. Charles John A. born.

1781   Eliza Hancock (George A.'s niece) m. Comte de
       Feuillide (guillotined 1794).

1782   C. E. A. and J. A. with Mrs. Cawley at Oxford; later
       at Southampton.

1783   Oct. Jane Cooper (Leigh), Mrs. A.'s sister, died.

1784 or 5   C. E. A. and J. A. leave the Abbey School,
       Reading.

1786   Egerton Brydges at Deane Parsonage. *Letters*,
       p. 105 note.

1788   July. C. E. A. and J. A. with parents at Sevenoaks.
       Life 58.

1791   27 Dec. Edward A. m. Elizabeth Bridges (d. 1808).

1792   27 Mar. James A. m. Anne Mathew (d. 3 May 1795).
       ? Aug. C. E. A. at Rowling. *Life* 62.

       Sept. C. E. A. and J. A. at Ibthorp. *Life* 62.

       11 Dec. Jane Cooper (Mrs. A.'s niece) m. Tom
       Williams (see 1798).

1793   23 Jan. Fanny Austen (Knight 1812) born.

---

[1] The Letters are referred to by the number in my edition
(Letter 40) or by my pages (*Letters*, p. 40).

14 Mar. Edward Cooper (Mrs. A.'s nephew) m. Caroline Lybbe Powys.

15 Apr. Anna A. born (Lefroy 1814).

? Dec. C. E. A. and J. A. at Southampton. *Letters*, p. 236.

1794 Feb. Comte de Feuillide guillotined.

? Summer–Oct. C. E. A. and J. A. in Kent.

Thomas Knight died.

1795 *Elinor and Marianne* written. *Life* 80.

C. E. A. engaged to Thomas Fowle (d. 1797).

Tom Lefroy at Ashe. *Letters*, pp. 3, 6, 27.

1796 Jan. C. E. A. at Kintbury (Letters 1–2).

Aug. J. A. in Cork St. (Letter 3).

Sept. J. A. at Rowling (Letters 4–7).

Oct. *First Impressions* begun (finished Aug. 1797).

1797 17 Jan. James A. m.(2) Mary Lloyd.

Feb. Thomas Fowle, C. E. A.'s fiancé, died.

Nov. C. E. A. and J. A. and mother with Leigh Perrots at Paragon, Bath. *Letters*, pp. 26, 59, 60, 148. *Life* 106.

Nov. *Sense and Sensibility* begun. *First Impressions* offered to Cadell.

31 Dec. Henry A. m. Eliza de Feuillide (d. 1813) (see 1794).

Mrs. Knight made over Godmersham to Edward A.

1797–8 *Northanger Abbey* (*Susan*) written.

1798 9 Aug. Jane Williams (see 1792) died.

Late Aug. C. E. A. and J. A. at Godmersham, *Letters*, p. 33, where C. E. A. remained till March 1799, *Letters*, p. 58.

23 Oct. J. A. and mother left Godmersham, *Letters*, p. 20 (Letter 9).

Oct.–Dec. C. E. A. at Godmersham (Letters 10–16).

17 Nov. James Edward Austen (Leigh 1837) born.

Samuel Blackall in Hampshire, *Letters*, p. 28; *Life* 86.

1799 Jan.–Mar. C. E. A. at Godmersham (see 1798) (Letters 17–18).

Feb. J. A. at Ibthorp? *Letters*, p. 58.

Mar. Martha Lloyd at Steventon? *Letters*, p. 58.

May–June. J. A. and mother with the Edward A.'s at 13 Queen Square, Bath (Letters 19–22).

Summer. J. A. at Godmersham? *Letters*, p. 50.

1800 25 Oct.–30 Nov. (and later?). C. E. A. at Godmersham. *Life* 156 (Letters 23–5, 27–8).

Nov. J. A. at Ibthorp.

1801 Jan.–Feb. C. E. A. at Godmersham (see 1800) (Letters 29–33).

Feb. C. E. A. with Henry in Upper Berkeley St. J. A. at Manydown (Letter 34).

May. J. A. and mother in Paragon, Bath; C. E. A. at Ibthorp and Kintbury (Letters 35–8).

Summer. C. E. A. and J. A. with parents at Sidmouth. *Letters*, pp. 101, 107, 118, 132. *Life* 90, 172; Thomson, *Survey* 202.

Autumn. The Austens settled at 4 Sydney Terrace, Bath. *Life* 172.

Hastings, son of Eliza de Feuillide (now Mrs. H. A.) died.

1802 Summer. C. E. A. and J. A. with parents at Dawlish and Teignmouth. *Letters*, pp. 85, 393. *Life* 173.

Nov.–Dec. C. E. A. and J. A. at Steventon and Manydown. Harris Bigg-Wither proposed to J. A. *Life* 92.

[Mrs. James Austen's diary supplies exact information.

1 Sept. C. E. A. and J. A. reached Steventon.

3 Sept. They left for Kent.

28 Oct. They returned to Steventon.

25 Nov. They left for Manydown.

3 Dec. They returned to Steventon.

4 Dec. They left for Bath.]

1803   Spring. *Susan* (*Northanger Abbey*) sold to Crosby & Co.

? J. A. at Ramsgate. *Letters*, p. 351. *Life* 174.

5 Nov. J. A. (and C. E. A.?) at Lyme. *Letters*, p. 216.

? *The Watsons* (date of watermark).

1804   Summer. J. A. and Henry, 'rambles'. *Letters*, p. 153.

Sept. J. A. and parents at Lyme. C. E. A. at Weymouth and Ibthorp. *Letters*, p. 138 (Letter 39).

16 Dec. Mrs. Lefroy killed.

1805   21 Jan. George A. died at 27 Green Park Buildings, Bath (Letters 40–2).

April. J. A. and mother at 25 Gay St., Bath; 'intended partnership' with Martha Lloyd, *Letters*, pp. 157, 170. C. E. A. at Ibthorp (Letters 43–4).

Aug. C. E. A. and J. A. at Godmersham and Goodnestone (but not together; Letters 45–7).

? *Lady Susan* (date of watermark).

Caroline A. born.

1806   Apr. Austens in Trim St., Bath. *Life* 191.

2 July. Austens leave Bath for Clifton, *Letters*, p. 208, Adlestrop and (Aug.) Stoneleigh. *Life* 194, 196.

24 July. Frank A. m. Mary Gibson (d. 1823).

Autumn. Austens and Martha join the Frank A.'s in lodgings in Southampton. *Life* 197.

1807   Jan.–Mar. C. E. A. at Godmersham, *Letters*, p. 183 (Letters 48–50).

Mar. Austens move into Castle Square, Southampton. *Letters*, pp. 178, 183; *Life* 203.

1 May. Charles A. m. Frances Palmer (d. 1814).

Sept. C. E. A. and J. A. and mother at Chawton House. Brabourne ii. 116.

1808 4–25 Feb. C. E. A. and J. A. with the James A.'s at Steventon, leaving 25 Feb. for Kintbury.

June. J. A. at Brompton with the Henry A.'s. *Letters*, pp. 191, 197, 209. J. A. and the James A.'s at Godmersham (Letters 51–4).

Oct.–Dec. C. E. A. at Godmersham (Letters 55–62).

10 Oct. Mrs. Edward A. died.

Oct. The Chawton plan. *Letters*, p. 229.

22 Dec. Cassandra (Cassy), d. of Charles A., born.

1809 Jan.–Feb. C. E. A. at Godmersham. *Life* 220 (Letters 63–6).

Apr. Correspondence with Crosby about *Susan*.

Apr. The Austens left Southampton for Bookham and Godmersham. *Letters*, pp. 246, 336.

26 July. First letter from Chawton (Letter 68).

1811 Feb. *Mansfield Park* begun (finished soon after June 1813).

Apr. J. A. in Sloane St. with the Henry A.'s (Letters 69–71).

Apr.–June. C. E. A. at Godmersham (Letters 72–4).

2–9 May. J. A. at Streatham with the Hills. *Letters*, pp. 271, 277.

Nov. *Sense and Sensibility: A Novel. In three volumes. By a Lady.* T. Egerton.

1812 Apr. Edward A. and Fanny at Chawton House. *Life* 256.

June. J. A. and mother at Steventon. *Life* 256.

14 Oct. Mrs. Thomas Knight died.

Nov. *Pride and Prejudice* sold to Egerton. *Letters*, p. 501. Edward A. at Chawton Cottage; takes the name of Knight. *Letters*, p. 500.

1813 Jan.–Feb. C. E. A. at Steventon and Manydown (Letters 75–8).

Jan. *Pride and Prejudice: A Novel. In three volumes. By the Author of 'Sense and Sensibility'*. T. Egerton.

Apr.–Sept. The Edward Knights at Chawton House. *Letters*, pp. 337, 341.

25 Apr. Mrs. Henry Austen died.

May. J. A. in Sloane St. with Henry (Letters 79–80).

? Aug. Henry A. at Daylesford with Warren Hastings. *Letters*, p. 320.

15–16 Sept. J. A. in Henrietta St. with Henry (Letters 82–3).

17 Sept.–13 Nov. J. A. at Godmersham (for the first time since 1809, *Letters*, p. 336). *Life* 291 (Letters 84–91).

Oct.–Nov. C. E. A. in Henrietta St.

Nov. *Sense and Sensibility*, second edition. *Pride and Prejudice*, second edition.

1814   21 Jan. *Emma* begun (finished 29 Mar. 1815).

Mar. J. A. in Henrietta St. and ? at Streatham. *Letters*, pp. 383, 387 (Letters 92–4).

May. *Mansfield Park: A Novel. In three volumes. By the Author of 'Sense and Sensibility' and 'Pride and Prejudice'*. T. Egerton.

June. C. E. A. in Henrietta St. The Edward A.'s at Chawton House. *Letters*, pp. 388, 390 (Letters 96–7).

24 June. J. A. at Bookham with the Cookes. *Letters*, pp. 389, 391.

Aug. J. A. in Hans Place with Henry (Letter 99).

6 Sept. Mrs. Charles A. died.

8 Nov. Anna A. m. Benjamin Lefroy.

Nov.–5 Dec. J. A. in Hans Place. *Letters*, p. 418 (Letters 105–9).

26 Dec.–?14 Jan. 1815. C. E. A. and J. A. at

Winchester (with Mrs. Heathcote) and Steventon. *Bellas MS.*

1815   Summer or Autumn. *Persuasion* begun (finished Aug. 1816).

4 Oct.–16 Dec. J. A. in Hans Place. *Letters*, pp. 424, 447 (Letters 111–22).

Nov. Edward Knight at Chawton. *Letters*, pp. 434, 440; *Life* 314.

Oct.–Nov. The Frank A.'s at Chawton House. *Letters*, pp. 427, 438.

Dec. *Emma: A Novel. In three volumes. By the Author of 'Pride and Prejudice', &c. &c.* John Murray. 1816.

Raison et Sensibilité, ou Les Deux Manières d'Aimer, traduit librement de l'anglais, par Mme Isabelle de Montolieu. Paris. Reprinted 1828.

1816   Mar. *Quarterly Review* ('October 1815') containing Scott's review of *Emma. Letters*, p. 453 note.

23 Mar. Henry A. bankrupt.

May. C. E. A. and J. A. at Cheltenham. *Life* 334.

Sept. C. E. A. at Cheltenham (Letters 132–3).

1816–17   The Frank A.'s at Alton.

1816   *Mansfield Park*, second edition.

July. Conclusion of *Persuasion* in its original form.

Le Parc de Mansfield, ou Les Trois Cousines, par l'auteur de Raison et Sensibilité, ou Les Deux Manières d'Aimer; d'Orgueil et Préjugé, etc. Traduit de l'Anglais, par M. Henri V*******n. (Villemain). Paris.

La Nouvelle Emma, ou les Caractères Anglais du Siècle, par l'auteur d'Orgueil et Préjugé, etc. etc. Traduit de l'Anglais. Paris.

1817   27 Jan.–18 Mar. Composition of 'Sanditon'.

28 Mar. James Leigh Perrot (Mrs. A.'s brother) died.

27 Apr. J. A. made her will.

24 May. C. E. A. and J. A. went to College St., Winchester. *Letters*, p. 496.

18 July. J. A. died.

Pride and Prejudice, third edition.

? Dec. *Northanger Abbey: and Persuasion. By the Author of 'Pride and Prejudice', 'Mansfield-Park', &c. With a Biographical Notice of the Author.* John Murray. 1818.

1819 James A. died.

1820 Fanny Knight m. Sir Edward Knatchbull.

1821 *La Famille Elliot, ou l'ancienne Inclination, traduction libre de l'anglais d'un roman posthume de Miss Jane Austen, auteur de Raison et Sensibilité, d'Orgueil et Préjugé, d'Emma, de Mansfield-Parc, etc. Par Mme. de Montolieu.* Paris. Reprinted 1828.

1822 *Orgueil et Préjugé. Par l'Auteur de Raison et Sensibilité. Traduit de l'anglois.* Paris.

Orgueil et Prévention, Par l'Auteur de Raison et Sensibilité; traduit de l'anglais Par Mlle E . . . .*** (Éloise Perks). Paris.

1824 *L'Abbaye de Northanger; Traduit de l'anglais de Jeanne Austen, auteur d'Orgueil et Préjugé, du Parc de Mansfield, de la Famille Elliot, de la Nouvelle Emma, etc. Par Mme. Hyacinthe de F***** (Ferrières). Paris.

1827 Mrs. Austen (born 1739) died.

1828 Frank A. m.(2) Martha Lloyd.

1832–3 *Elizabeth Bennet; or, Pride and Prejudice*—and the other novels. Philadelphia.

1833 Bentley's collected edition, reprinted 1837, 1866, 1869, 1878–9, 1882.

1843 Lady (Francis) Austen (Martha Lloyd) died.

1845 C. E. A. died.

1850 Henry A. died.

1852 Edward Knight died.
      Charles A. died.

1865 Sir Francis A. died.
      Recollections of the Vine Hunt by J. E. Austen Leigh.

1870 *Memoir* of J. A. by her nephew James Edward Austen
      Leigh (see 1871).

1871 Second edition of the *Memoir* with *Lady Susan*, *The
      Watsons*, and the cancelled chapter of *Persuasion*.

1884 *Letters of Jane Austen* edited by her great-nephew
      Lord Brabourne.

1892 Dent's edition of the novels.

1902 *Jane Austen, her Homes and her Friends*, by Constance
      Hill.

1906 *Jane Austen's Sailor Brothers* by J. H. and E. C. Hub-
      back, first publication of letters to Frank A.

1911 *Chawton Manor* by W. Austen Leigh and M. G.
      Knight.

1913 *Life and Letters of Jane Austen* by W. and R. A.
      Austen Leigh. Second edition 1913. Out of print.

1920 *Personal Aspects of Jane Austen* by Mary Augusta
      Austen Leigh.

1922 *Love and Freindship* (Vol. II of *Juvenilia*) published.

1923 Oxford edition of the novels by R. W. Chapman.
      Reprinted 1926, 1933, and later.

1925 *Sanditon* published.

1926 *Two Chapters of Persuasion* reprinted from the original.
      Plan of a Novel, Opinions on *Mansfield Park* and *Emma*,
      &c., reprinted or first printed from the originals.

1927 *The Watsons* reprinted from the original (see 1871).

1928 *Lady Susan* reprinted from the original (see 1871).

1932 *Letters of Jane Austen* edited by R. W. Chapman.

1933 *Volume the First* (of *Juvenilia*) published.

NOTES ON THE NOVELS

HEREDITY

I HAVE wondered that Jane Austen's enemies have never, to my knowledge, fastened on what may seem a grave weakness: her defiance of the probabilities of heredity. This stares us in the face at Longbourn, where the family circle comprises extremes of virtue and vice, wit and pedantry, shrewdness and folly. Upon what genetic hypothesis was this miscellany (in five volumes) founded? I am no biologist, and not much of a novel-reader; my very fallible impression is that the nineteenth-century novelists were not much alive to the problems of heredity, which their successors in this century have found so rewarding. It is just possible that Jane Austen never looked at her families in this light.

But let us collect the evidence. Mrs. Dashwood enters the stage as a widow, and we learn little of her husband. We might draw inferences from the character of Mr. John Dashwood, but they would not help us; for the three Dashwood girls, though two of them are anti-thetical, have neither parsimony nor any other moral failing. Mr. Bennet, manifestly, fell in love with a beautiful child, and learned too late into what an abyss of vulgar folly he had lowered himself. The results we have already glanced at. General Tilney is a widower. Of his wife we know that her memory was cherished by his virtuous son and his virtuous daughter. Captain Tilney is only sketched, but he seems his father's son. The problem in *Mansfield Park* is more complex. We have first the three Ward sisters, who are strikingly disparate. The placid nullity of Lady Bertram has its counterpart in the incompetence of her sister Price, whose querulous nature has, in turn, some affinity with sister Norris's bad temper. But the gulf yawns wide between Lady Bertram and that female Iago Mrs. Norris, whose only merit is her infatuation with the nieces who had inherited some of her vices. The Bertram children, again, while they are all men and women of parts (one wonders, whence derived), are morally very unlike; three goats to one sheep. Mr. Woodhouse, a widower, is mirrored in his elder daughter, and sharply contradicted by his younger daughter; the late Mrs. Woodhouse perhaps resolves the problem. Finally we have Sir Walter Elliot, again a widower, of whose wife we know that she needed no forgiveness except for 'the youthful indiscretion that made her Lady Elliot'. Here we contrast the sublime selfishness of Sir Walter, two of his daughters, and his cousin's son, with the almost culpable self-abnegation of his other daughter, who no doubt 'took after' her mother.

Jane Austen's experience of families was not narrow. Her own family was unusually rich in variations and contrasts. As she grew older she became intimate with a number of large families. We may be sure that family likenesses and unlikenesses, moral as well as physical, were often canvassed in conversation with Cassandra or with Martha Lloyd. It is natural to suppose that she would apply the same critical sympathy to the creatures of her invention.

The first fact that strikes me is that in only two of the six novels is the central family furnished with two living parents. The second is that in all, except perhaps *Sense and Sensibility*, we know or can infer a marked disparity, moral or intellectual or both, between the partners. I mention, to reject it, the theory that she was not interested in married happiness, or was interested in married life only as it gave opportunity to her satiric talent. It is sufficient to recall the case of Admiral and Mrs. Croft, a charming picture of connubial bliss; or Emma's genius for matchmaking; or Captain Harville's views on the Benwick–Musgrove marriage:

I confess that I do think there is a disparity, too great a disparity, and in a point no less essential than mind.[1]

Yet the contrast between the two generations, between the ill-assorted matches contracted before the action of the novels begins and the marriage of true minds, a harmony in diversity, that she plans for her heroes and heroines, is very marked. It is true, of course, that a novelist needs plenty of light and shade, and is entitled to strain probability to get it. It is equally true that romantic convention demanded that a novel should end on a prospect of lifelong felicity,[2] and Jane Austen loved her young people too much to allow any shadow to fall on their future. But the disparities go further, I think, than is to be explained as common novelists' licence. Jane Austen's novels are, in a quite exceptional degree—

[1] *Persuasion*, ch. 21 (182).

[2] She was not prepared to take this for granted. Jane Fairfax was too good for Frank Churchill; and Jane Austen told her intimates that Mrs. Frank Churchill died young.

as some of her titles indicate—studies in moral contrasts. The soft colour-washes of her delicate brush are only just sufficient to mitigate the sharp clash of black and white that her characters exhibit, even within the limits of a single family. It may well be, I think, that she deliberately gave herself a flying start, from ill-assorted parents or by killing one parent in advance and so leaving his or her character to be inferred.

I do not suggest that any of the novels is a conscious study of heredity as such. For that, if knowledge and memory serve me, the palm must be given, among nineteenth-century novelists, to Trollope. I know nothing more delicate in its kind than the exquisite blend, in *The Duke's Children*—Lord Silverbridge, Lord Gerald Palliser, and Lady Mary Palliser—of qualities derived from the Duke of Omnium and qualities derived from their mother, best known to all of us as Lady Glencora.

IMPLICATION

I will pivot on *Pride and Prejudice* a note on one aspect of Jane Austen's economy: her rigid avoidance of anything outside her experience or her chosen subject. It has been noted[1] that she hardly ever leaves two of her young men alone together. She did not know just what they would say. This is, of course, a limitation, indeed a serious one. But she was a woman, belonging to a strict sect of the upper middle class; she had not the opportunities of a George Eliot. Nor had she that power of divination which allowed Trollope to follow young

[1] I believe by myself. It first appeared in print, I think, in something of Walter Raleigh; but he had it from me.

women to a common bedroom—or at least as far as the keyhole—and report their talk. But a limitation, if by circumstance or by nature it is ineluctable, should be obeyed, not evaded; and Jane Austen's dexterity is such that the disadvantage is hardly perceived. She knew enough of her young men for her own purpose, and perhaps rather more than the girls did who were to marry them.

So, in *Pride and Prejudice*, we see Darcy at a ball; on a visit to his friend and his friend's sisters, or to his noble aunt; calling at Hunsford parsonage. His more masculine or more public activities are merely reported, oftener merely hinted. But I think we can, by a legitimate use of the imagination, get a glimpse of these activities. We can see him, for instance, in his library, of which he could not conceive the neglect 'in times like these'; walking in the grounds of Pemberley, dispensing orders and charity; in Bingley's picture of him as an 'awful object . . . at his own house . . . of a Sunday evening when he has nothing to do'. His name, Fitzwilliam Darcy, his mother's, Lady Anne, and the grandeurs of Pemberley, identify him as a Northern magnate at a time when territorial influence, especially in the wide spaces of the North, was still all-powerful. I find it easy to jump a few hurdles and to see him as a public character: answering an invitation to stand for the county, or dining with the Archbishop of York.

Jane Austen's letters tell us a good deal of this her 'own darling child', which we may believe remained her favourite when she had moved on to more serious or more ambitious work. They give only one glimpse of her hero, which I cannot resist, though it has already been mentioned.[1] She went to an exhibition in London, and was disappointed to find no portrait of Elizabeth. She could only suppose that Darcy would not allow it to be 'exposed to the public eye. I can imagine he would have that sort of feeling—that mixture of Love, Pride, and Delicacy.' This is a good illustration of Jane Austen's habit (the records are tantalizing) of letting her imagination work—but not for publication—outside the frame of her picture. It gives moreover a pleasing instance of the 'proper' pride to which Elizabeth's influence had confined her lover and husband.

PLOT

Perhaps the most damaging criticism ever made of Jane Austen as a novelist is Mr. Garrod's—that she had but one plot. In five of the six novels we have a village, or something like it: the Dashwoods' cottage in Devonshire, Meryton, Mansfield Park, Highbury, Kellynch. In this village lives a marriageable maiden: Marianne, Elizabeth, Fanny, Emma, Anne. To this village comes, on various pretexts, an eligible bachelor: a neighbouring Willoughby, a transient Darcy, a visiting Crawford, a speciously related Churchill, a Wentworth on leave from the King's service. The exception is *Northanger Abbey*, where both parties are drawn from outside into the vortex of Bath. Mr. Garrod might have added that each heroine is furnished with a pendant, rival, or foil; Marianne with Eleanor, Elizabeth with Jane, Catherine with Isabella, Fanny with Mary, Emma with Jane; Anne

[1] Pp. 80, 123.

Elliot, whose case does not fit this scheme quite neatly, has two foils to set off her beauty: call her Cordelia, and Miss Elliot assumes the proportions of Goneril, if Mary Musgrove is an inadequate Regan.

I elaborate this point for its own interest, and because the Devil's advocate deserves a hearing. But the monotony of this parallelism seems hardly to have been noticed, which may suggest that it does not much matter. I do not think that plot, as plot, ever does much matter, provided it gives a reasonably probable and symmetrical framework within which character and sentiment can have free play. Jane Austen's straight-waistcoats do not seem to hamper the free movement of her limbs. That is notoriously true of traditional conventions; unconventional art is chaos, and so should not be called art. I do not see why the same may not hold good of a personal convention; whether deliberately chosen or due to some poverty of invention.

Anthony Trollope was bad at construction; so much so that he once employed a friend to make a plot for him. The result was, almost always, the jumble we know, and affectionately condone. He began with people. Having got to know them, he seized his pen and let it take him as it would; in any direction, no matter whether with the hounds or not, so long as the pace was good. (His foxhunting passion compels the simile.) Jane Austen's methods must have been very different. But I do not think there is anything to show how she worked, except that she worked rather slowly and with inexhaustible patience. The manuscripts, profusely corrected *currente calamo*, here confirm her own account of the matter.

Her output was nonetheless substantial. *Mansfield Park* was begun about February 1811 and finished in little more than two years, part of which time was probably spent in 'lopping and cropping' *Pride and Prejudice*. *Emma* was begun and finished in fourteen months in 1814–15. In the short time that remained of health, *Persuasion* was written and *Sanditon* well begun.

LOVE AND MARRIAGE

Lord David Cecil has stated Jane Austen's view of love and marriage in one sentence, which needs no addition. 'It was wrong to marry for money, but it was silly to marry without it.' But the mercenary view of marriage is proclaimed by many of her people, and practised by even more. Charlotte Lucas, Elizabeth Bennet's friend, defends her acceptance of the egregious Collins. Lady Bertram holds it to be Fanny's 'duty' to accept Crawford; Sir Thomas himself, though he wraps up the doctrine in specious circumlocution, acts on it ruthlessly. The wicked people of course—General Tilney, Mary Crawford, and a host besides—take it for granted. It is to be remembered, in extenuation, that the alternative to marriage, for a penniless woman, was being a governess: a calling which Jane Eyre and Jane Fairfax, for once in accord, regard as slavery.

Only less odious, in our eyes, than the mercenary view is the snobbish view; and this Jane Austen comes much nearer to condoning. She accepts it as right and proper that Darcy should struggle—though she rejoices that he 'struggled in vain'[1]—before bridging the enormous

[1] *Pride and Prejudice*, ch. 35 (p. 189).

social gulf that yawned between him and Mrs. Bennet's daughter. Here, again, some historical sense is necessary to our understanding. We must remember that the doctrine which Johnson calls subordination was still accepted by the great majority of good and sensible people; it had been impugned only by those whom Jane Austen classes as 'Disciples of Godwin'.[1]

These erroneous doctrines are so pervasive in her books that many people have accepted them as her own. An extreme instance is an interpretation of *Pride and Prejudice* which was, and I fear still is, quite common: the view that Elizabeth was first brought round by the sight of the wealth and grandeur of Pemberley. This is grotesque. But the belief that Jane Austen, like the rest of her class, was worldly and a snob might be buttressed by the fact that all her heroines *do* marry men who are either rich or in comfortable circumstances. She might retort that she is entitled, nay is bound, to secure them the felicity they deserve; and that in her time, when a baby once in eighteen months was a law of life, a good income was a condition of happiness.

To correct all these caveats, if I have over-stated them, it is only necessary to recall your attention to the words and conduct of those of Jane Austen's girls who are as good as they are pretty: to Elizabeth's repudiation of Collins, Fanny's of Crawford, Anne's of her crafty cousin. Their words are not less eloquent than their actions: Marianne's, when she contemns Colonel Brandon's advancing years and flannel waistcoats; Eliza-

---

[1] Letter of 21 May 1801. Emma, I think, *is* something of a snob; she is the only heroine who merits the name.

beth's when she censures her friend's calculating prudence; Anne's when she claims for her sex 'the privilege
. . . of loving longest when existence or when hope is
gone'.

Strange misconceptions are abroad on the subject of
Jane Austen and love. Her reticence has misled the most
acute of critics. My old friend Mr. E. M. Forster has
declared that 'She knows the facts; but they are not her
facts'. A wiser paradox was George Moore's, who
somewhere exclaims that Marianne Dashwood is the
only study of passion—'the burning human heart'—
in all our *prose* literature. The best example I recall of
Jane Austen's hint of the depth of her knowledge is in
Northanger Abbey, the scene in which Henry Tilney
catches Catherine Morland *in flagrante delicto*—in the
act of hunting for evidence of his father's ineffable guilt.
He scolds her, as you will remember; and his last words,
which dismiss her in tears, are 'Dearest Miss Morland,
what ideas have you been admitting?'[1] If you will look
at the passage again, I think you will see that those
words are the climax of a scene that vibrates with
passion.

Miss Mary Lascelles, with the finality she has taught
us to expect, has the last word on this matter when she
remarks that Jane Austen's lovers 'walk off the stage
into a cloud'—where it would be indecent to attempt to
follow them. You will find the same reticence in Henry
James; I recall an emotional exchange in *The Golden
Bowl*; it happens in a carriage, perhaps a cab; its intimacy is conveyed by a series of metaphors.

[1] Ch. 25 (p. 198).

MANSFIELD PARK

Many readers, I suspect, like myself, have found *Mansfield Park* the most difficult of the works, in the sense that it is there hardest to be sure of the writer's general intention. She wrote to her sister, at the outset, that she was 'going to take a new subject, ordination'. That is not what we should choose, if we had to describe the theme in a word or a phrase. Some would say, perhaps, Love and Friendship, or Love and Selfishness, or Riches and Poverty. But it is true that the incompatibility of Edmund and Mary, which is focal to the plot, arises largely out of his choice of a profession too unambitious to content her. My own term, if I were confined to one, would be Environment. The ostensible moral of the book, which is almost blatantly didactic, is that education, religious and moral, is omnipotent over character. It is true that this theory is oftenest voiced by the more priggish of the persons: solemn Sir Thomas, his virtuous son, and his pensive niece. But it is plainly endorsed by their author, who was perhaps at this time too much under the influence of one of her favourite divines or secular moralists.

This is a grave fault, and I do not find it in the other books. Fortunately the disease is not mortal. Jane Austen's satiric genius is at hand to correct her preconceptions. What she tells us of her persons is vitiated by this one-sided theory. But the persons themselves act and talk naturally, exhibiting just that share of original sin with which nature—helped or hindered, no doubt, by their upbringing—had endowed them.

This brings me to the vexed question of the Crawfords. It is a common view that Jane Austen vacillated, finally cutting the knot with the blunt razor of elopement and adultery. I cannot bring myself to accept this. If Jane Austen had made such a muddle of a book I think she must have known it; she was incapable of self-deception. I do not think she would have published her book unless she could clear up the mess.[1]

Lord David Cecil in his Leslie Stephen lecture, the best short view known to me of Jane Austen's work, states the common opinion, less crudely than I have stated it here. Henry Crawford was designed as the villain, came to life as a sympathetic character, and was driven back to sinful courses by an arbitrary use of his author's prerogative, and so was made to act 'in a manner wholly inconsistent with the rest of his character'. I suggest that it is Lord David, not Jane Austen, who is blinded by Henry's all but irresistible charm.

It is a sound rule, in criticism of a supreme artist, to hold him innocent until his guilt is proved.[2] Let him at least be heard in defence. Jane Austen, I believe, lays all her cards on the table in that famous chapter which begins 'Let other pens dwell on guilt and misery'. She in fact dwells on them herself, briefly but adequately.

---

[1] She never brought herself to the point of publishing *Northanger Abbey*, though she prepared it for publication in 1803; in 1817 she wrote that 'Miss Catherine is put upon the Shelve for the present, and I do not know that she will ever come out'.

[2] John Cann Bailey, a learned and catholic critic, admired Jane Austen enough to write a book about her, in which he again and again shows himself content to believe that she did not know the elements of her job.

If Edmund had married Mary, as he must have done if his eyes had not been opened by her cynical condonation of the elopement, Fanny's moral rectitude would have enabled her to suppress her passion, and every thing— and every body—would have conspired to drive her into Henry's arms.

All this I am bound by my premises to accept—as Jane Austen's intention, not as necessarily true to life. Otherwise thought is free. What, then, would Fanny have found in Henry? I believe that she would have found what was always there: intellect, charm, and boundless good humour, tempering a cold-blooded cynical selfishness. I cannot accept Jane Austen's *theory* that he was 'ruined by early independence and bad domestic example'; he was born a rake, and the Admiral's living in sin did not make him one. But I do accept her *fact*: that he 'indulged in the freaks of a cold-blooded vanity a little too long'. I am confident that Jane Austen could have told us, if she had chosen, just where he kept his mistress. That lady would have been discarded, I daresay, on his marriage; and when he tired of Fanny, he would have been uniformly kind and courteous, and would have kept his affairs discreetly in the background. More than that I cannot give him. The elopement, as described, might come straight out of Horace Walpole's letters, and is to me perfectly credible.

Henry's sister, too, is all of a piece: bound, as her brother was not bound, by prudential restraints, but of the same base metal; abounding in kindness, so it cost her nothing; a heartless, selfish flirt.

It remains to state the evidence in greater detail. I

think that Jane Austen knew what she was about. She had, at least, searched her conscience, and believed herself to have dealt even-handed justice to her villains, just as (it has often been remarked) she is just to that most odious of her characters, Mrs. Norris. Henry's first design was to fill an idle fortnight by 'making a small hole in Fanny Price's heart'. Circumstances soon show it worth piercing. Fanny's sailor brother comes on the scene, and her enthusiastic devotion makes 'a picture which Henry Crawford had moral taste enough to value'.[1] He is already caught; 'a fortnight was not enough. His stay became indefinite.' 'Moral taste'; the phrase is arresting. Later, the judgement is elaborated. Henry describes Fanny's virtues to his sister, and the author sums up.

Henry Crawford had too much sense not to feel the worth of good principles in a wife, though he was too little accustomed to serious reflection to know them by their proper name; but when he talked of her having such a steadiness and regularity of conduct, such a high notion of honour, and such an observance of decorum as might warrant any man in the fullest dependence on her faith and integrity, he expressed what was inspired by the knowledge of her being well principled and religious.[2]

Jane Austen's attitude to private theatricals in general, and to Lovers' Vows in particular, has puzzled many readers. She did not disapprove of the theatre; like Edmund Bertram, she was a lover of good, 'hardened', professional acting. She can hardly have come to condemn amateur acting, which her family had practised,

[1] Ch. 37 (p. 235).   [2] Ch. 43 (p. 294).

under the tuition of her brilliant cousin, Madame de Feuillide, in the rectory barn at Steventon. She can hardly have been much shocked by the ridiculous German play. It deals indeed with illegitimacy; but it had been adapted to the English taste by Mrs. Inchbald, and Jane Austen would have agreed with Mrs. Norris that anything too 'warm' could be readily expunged.

The scruples stated by the virtuous characters, and endorsed by their author, are mainly domestic and topical. Edmund does state a case against ladies' and gentlemen's making fools of themselves before half the county; but that motive is not much stressed. Sir Thomas was in the West Indies; his predictable reprobation, however based, was enough to condemn the scheme. Worse than this, the casting of the play made it clear that there must be awkward situations and dangerous propinquities; for some of the *dramatis personae* knew that others of them were already skating on thin ice. Mary herself was taken aback when called on to 'vamp' Edmund as the virtuous Anhalt, and suggested drastic cuts. And it was easily foreseen that the juxtaposition of Henry Crawford with either of the Bertram girls as his mother, 'trying not to embrace', must disconcert poor Rushworth, and might have grave results—entanglements that could not be named.

There is one more point. The class to which Jane Austen and her Bertrams belonged regarded the aristocracy with suspicious hostility. Now *Lovers' Vows* was under that cloud; it was introduced by an Hon. John Yates (aristocratic counterpart of John Thorpe) from a country-house performance the cast of which had included a duke. But dukes as a class, and baronets and country parsons as a class, were then remote from each other; the former class despised its inferiors, and the inferiors retorted with moral reprobation.[1]

The affair of *Lovers' Vows* reminds me to call attention to a minor technical point. Each of Jane Austen's novels, published in her lifetime, was in three volumes. The division was not left to the printer; it was part, and a not wholly unimportant part, of the design. It tends to compose, at least to define, any natural divisions of the story. These landmarks have been unhappily destroyed in almost all modern editions. The three volumes of *Mansfield Park* might perhaps be denoted thus: Volume I, Private Theatricals; Volume II, Henry's courtship of Fanny; Volume III, her banishment to Portsmouth, Henry's pursuit of her there, the catastrophe (off stage), and the climax. How dramatic a preliminary or minor climax may be is well shown in the last page of Volume I, which rings down the curtain on the last rehearsal:

They . . . had proceeded some way, when the door . . . was thrown open, and Julia appearing at it, with a face all aghast, exclaimed, 'My father is come! He is in the hall at this moment.'

Mansfield Park is, I think, the least 'sympathetic' of the novels; more than any of the rest, it enables us to understand the critics who find Jane Austen herself uncongenial. It has none of the faults that are obvious enough elsewhere: it has not the crudity of *Sense and*

[1] See p. 26.

Sensibility, nor the element of caricature that we have to overlook in Mary Bennet and Mr. Collins and Lady Catherine, nor the creaking machinery that distresses lovers of *Persuasion*. But it has a certain constraint, which is not wholly dramatic: I had almost said, a moral harshness. It is, on the other hand, in some respects the most impressive of the novels: the most compelling, most dominant. In *Mansfield Park* alone does Jane Austen tread the confines of tragedy.

You will remember that Sir Thomas, back from Antigua, is constrained to see that his elder daughter has engaged herself to a man whom she cannot possibly love, or even respect. He begs her to think again, and offers his support if she wishes to break off the engagement. Maria, after only 'a moment's struggle', is able to reply, with a composure equal to her father's, that 'she could not have a doubt of her happiness'. Then follows this analysis:

Henry Crawford had destroyed her happiness, but he should not know that he had done it; he should not destroy her credit, her appearance, her prosperity too. He should not have to think of her as pining in the retirement of Mansfield for *him*, rejecting Sotherton and London, independence and splendour for *his* sake. Independence was more needful than ever; the want of it at Mansfield more sensibly felt. She was less and less able to endure the restraint which her father imposed. The liberty which his absence had given was now become absolutely necessary. She must escape from him and Mansfield as soon as possible, and find consolation in fortune and consequence, bustle and the world, for a wounded spirit. Her mind was quite determined and varied not.

To such feelings, delay, even the delay of much preparation, would have been an evil, and Mr. Rushworth could hardly be more impatient for the marriage than herself. In all the important preparations of the mind she was complete; being prepared for matrimony by an hatred of home, restraint, and tranquility; by the misery of disappointed affection, and contempt of the man she was to marry. The rest might wait.[1]

EMMA

Emma is, I think, clearly Jane Austen's masterpiece. I have a friend who in his younger days saw a great deal of the late Lord Rosebery, a formidable person. Once the old man said 'I am going to ask a question. Of course *Tom Jones* is the best English novel; what do you say is the next best?' My friend replied 'I shall be bold and say *Emma*'. 'Quite right!' Thus I am in good company. Here I interject that I am, and think we should all be, rather impatient of putting works of art into class-lists; in Macaulay this ordering of merit became a vice. But the temptation to rank *Emma* is irresistible. I do not put it first because the major characters most engage our affections. Perhaps some elderly people may put George Knightley at the head of their list (his name *was* George, though we are hardly allowed to know it); all must agree that he is a perfect English gentleman; as perfect, I think, as Plantagenet Palliser, Duke of Omnium, though not near so great an achievement of creation. For myself, I retain a sneaking preference for Henry Tilney: for no better reason, perhaps, than that I find in him a resemblance to my youthful priggishness. But he has more wit than any of her young men except Henry Crawford.

[1] Ch. 21 (p. 202).

Emma herself, I suppose, is no one's favourite. Her creator wrote, or said, 'I am going to take a heroine whom no one but myself will much like'.[1]

Some of the minor portraits are as good as any in the long gallery. Macaulay's parallel of Jane Austen and Shakespeare has I think done positive disservice to the lesser artist. But Miss Bates at least may be justly called Shakespearian; she is, on her own plane, comparable with Sir John himself.

But it is not on the ground of character that I base my claim. I find the supremacy of *Emma* in the matchless symmetry of its design, in the endless fascination of its technique, above all in the flow of the blood beneath the smooth polished skin: a flow of human sympathy and charity that beats with a steady pulse, rarely—but the more momentously—quickening to a throb that sets our own veins leaping in unison. I need only remind you of the agony of Box Hill—the climax of the scene is to me, after a score of readings, almost intolerable—or of that final climax when Emma learns, in two blinding flashes, that she has always been wrong and that she has never been wrong.

'As a friend!'—repeated Mr. Knightley.—'Emma, that I fear is a word—No, I have no wish—Stay, yes, why should I hesitate?—I have gone too far already for concealment.—Emma, I accept your offer—Extraordinary as it may seem, I accept it, and refer myself to you as a friend.—Tell me, then, have I no chance of ever succeeding?'

He stopped in his earnestness to look the question, and the expression of his eyes overpowered her.[2]

[1] *Memoir*, ch. 10.

[2] Compare the cancelled chapter of *Persuasion* (p. 258 in my

I need not quote more, I believe, to recall the whole to your memory: the nadir of Emma's romantic experience, and the zenith that so quickly followed.

Henry Austen applied to his sister, just dead, a famous passage from Donne:

> Her pure and eloquent blood
> Spoke in her cheeks, and so distinctly wrought,
> That one might almost say, her body thought.[1]

The lovely lines may with equal aptitude be quoted in praise of this consummation of her art.

Emma supplies me with my favourite example of what, in a remark on Jane Austen's letters, I have called the miracle of communication. To invoke the miraculous may be thought an abdication of the critic's office. But this kind of wizardry seems hitherto to have defied analysis, and I suppose we may say *omne ignotum pro miraculo*. Every reader—I say this, having tested it on readers not prone to literary nicety—remembers the wet July evening that followed Emma's crowning disillusionment. The briefest reminder will serve.

It darted through her, with the speed of an arrow, that Mr. Knightley must marry no one but herself! (408)

'Oh God! that I had never seen her' (i.e. Harriet Smith, 411).

Now if you look, as I once looked, for a description

edition), where Wentworth too proposes marriage mainly with his eyes. The repetition might make a part of her recorded dissatisfaction with her first draft. What replaced it—the scene at the White Hart—is no doubt an improvement, though the machinery is somewhat artificial. But the original is so good that it might well have satisfied even her fastidious taste.

[1] *The Second Anniversary.* See p. 31.

of that evening, you will almost say that it is not there. There is nothing but three curt, matter-of-fact sentences

> The evening of this day was very long, and melancholy, at Hartfield. The weather added what it could of gloom. A cold stormy rain set in, and nothing of July appeared but in the trees and shrubs, which the wind was despoiling, and the length of the day, which only made such cruel sights the longer visible.

No more than that. Yet the impression is ineffaceable.

Less important than these excellences, but to a professional even more seductive, is the technique that reveals itself in *Emma*, perhaps in *Emma* alone. More than twenty years ago I published an article on 'Jane Austen's Methods', in which I elaborated the view that in *Emma* we are hardly allowed to see anything except through the heroine's eyes; our vision is actually distorted by her faulty spectacles. I say hardly, because Mrs. Weston, for instance, supplies some facts. But this is scarcely an infraction of the dramatic method, for Mrs. Weston's contribution is no more than stage direction. The method stands, therefore, and is, in the year of Waterloo, portentous. When I wrote that article I had read Kipling's story *The Janeites*. You must let me inform or remind you of that remarkable blend of realism with criticism. The time is March 1918, before and during the Germans' last offensive; the place, the officers' mess in a battery of heavy guns; the persons, those officers, the drunken gentlemanranker who was their mess-waiter: all these, fanatical Janeites; the narrator, assistant mess-waiter, an intelligent and wholly illiterate cockney (note that, for it explains the lingo), who is compelled by his superior to read and memorize the novels, which he finds almost unintelligible and wholly devoid of interest.

The officers, all I think of civilian extraction, are on their favourite theme. One of them deplores Jane's having 'died barren'. Hear the sequel.

'I 'adnt noticed Macklin much, or I'd ha' seen 'e was bosko absoluto. Then 'e cut in, leanin' over a packin'-case with a face on 'im like a dead mackerel in the dark. "Pa-hardon me, Gents", Macklin says, "but this *is* a matter on which I *do* 'appen to be moderately well-informed. She *did* leave lawful issue in the shape of a son; an' his name was 'Enery James."'

Jane Austen's strict adherence to her rule more than once brings her to the brink of cheating—I do not apologize for the word, for *Emma* is among other things a detective story. Not long ago I discovered an example of this peccadillo that had eluded me as (I was gratified to find) it had eluded Miss Lascelles. Frank Churchill pays at last his long expected visit to Highbury. His proud father brings him to Hartfield. Mr. Weston, as Emma cannot fail to see, has already made a match of it. The young man plays up with delicate—not very delicate—flattery. At last

A reasonable visit paid, Mr. Weston began to move.—'He must be going. He had business at the Crown about his hay . . . but he need not hurry any body else.' His son, too well bred to hear the hint, rose immediately also.[1]

[1] Ch. 24 (p. 193).

and gave an elaborately mendacious explanation of a duty which must compel him to seek out a family named Barnes or Bates.

'Too well bred to hear the hint.' But Frank, of course, was eager to jump at any hint that would take him from the ostensible magnet to the real magnet. It is Emma who sees reluctance in his escape. I think the slip inadvertent; I acquit Jane Austen of deliberately throwing dust in our eyes.

NATURE

To those critics who assert that Jane Austen disliked fresh air, her apologists reply by pointing to a few isolated passages: notably to the rapturous delight of the Dashwood girls in the high wind that brought them acquainted with Willoughby, and the description in *Persuasion* of the beauties of Lyme. We all welcome these rare purplish patches. But I do not think we are entitled to expect them. The gentle rhapsody on Lyme —doubtless autobiographical—is not very unlike the digression into literary criticism that has been noted as an excrescence on *Northanger Abbey*. What we *are* entitled to expect, and shall find if we look, is casual, incidental hints, arising naturally out of the narrative or the dialogue. Such are Fanny Price's sage observation that 'this weather is all from the south', or the description of the walk on the Portsmouth ramparts:

The day was uncommonly lovely. It was really March; but it was April in its mild air, brisk soft wind, and bright sun, occasionally clouded for a minute; and everything looked so beautiful under the influence of such a sky, the effects of the shadows pursuing each other, on the ships at Spithead and the island beyond, with the ever-varying hues of the sea now at high water, dancing in its glee and dashing against the ramparts with so fine a sound, produced altogether such a combination of charms for Fanny, as made her gradually almost careless of the circumstances under which she felt them.

The circumstance was, you remember, that Crawford had compelled her to take his arm.

DEVELOPMENT: SANDITON

The differences between Jane Austen's first three novels and her last three are familiar, and are sufficiently explained by the lapse of time. They are indeed surprisingly less than we might expect between the work of a writer's early twenties and the same writer's late thirties. It would be fanciful to think of her as born to an early death; but she was, among novelists, unusually precocious. *Pride and Prejudice* is like Pallas Athene, who sprang full-armed from her father's head.

But what, if anything, can we say of the books she did not live to write? Those of her most prolific period show versatility rather than development; the themes, the force, the technique of *Mansfield Park*, *Emma*, and *Persuasion* are very different; but if they had been undated it would not be easy to place them in ordered time. For what was to come we are dependent on a single fragment of the novel, not named by its author, but traditionally known as *Sanditon*. We possess an early version, much corrected as it was written, of a

book which from the width of its canvass and its
leisurely procedure I guess to have been planned on the
scale of *Emma*. If that is so, then we have about half of
the first of three volumes. These are slender founda-
tions on which to build; but the attempt has been made.
Two tendencies can, I think, be discerned, which at first
sight seem to be at variance. The fragment has a certain roughness and harshness of satire, especially in
the characters of the hypochondriac brother and sisters,
of the bully Lady Denham, and above all of the wicked
baronet, which at its worst amounts to caricature; a
defect from which the later novels are almost free. This
might be due to failing powers; I doubt it. It is due in
part to lack of revision; she would have smoothed these
coarse strokes, so strikingly different from the mellow
pencillings of *Persuasion*. But a degree of savagery
would, I think, have persisted.

The other tendency is a matter of atmosphere, and is
more elusive. I cannot give my impression more per-
suasively than by quoting Mr. Forster, whose critical
reputation, if I have succeeded in damaging it a little in
earlier pages, I rejoice to restore to its true level.

He quotes a description of a view, which reached 'to
the sea, dancing and sparkling in sunshine and freshness', and this is his comment:

Not only does the sea dance in freshness, but another con-
figuration has been given to the earth, making it at once more
poetic and more definite. Sanditon gives out an atmosphere,
and also exists as a geographic and economic force. . . . The
change is . . . interesting because it took place in her mind—
that self-contained mind which had hitherto regarded the face

of the earth as a site for shrubberies and strawberry beds, and had denied it features of its own.

This does less than justice to the 'mind' of the six novels. But Mr. Forster has put his finger on something which is new, and which invites to speculation.

I am not yet clear to what conclusion speculation would lead me. But others besides myself, I find, have been called to attention by a scene in the last chapter, where the observant, critical Charlotte identifies a 'stolen interview' of 'secret lovers'. What she sees, as she walks, is 'a glimpse of something white and womanish'; and she sees it on 'a close, misty morning' and through a gap in the park paling. All the items of *chiaroscuro*—the mist, the treacherous fence, the ill-defined flutter of ribbons—add up to an effect which is as clearly deliberate as it is certainly novel.

STYLE

Jane Austen makes, I believe, only one reference to her style: when she writes of 'the playfulness and epigrammatism of the style' of *P.P.* (p. 81). There she is perhaps thinking chiefly of the dialogue, in which those qualities are conspicuous. All literate persons in that age were taught to be studious of 'style', even when, like Fanny Price, they were only writing a letter. But that meant little more than attention to grammar and stops. I doubt if J.A. was conscious of having a style of her own. Outside her dialogue it is not highly individual; it is just the ordinary correct English that, as Johnson had said, 'everyone now writes'. It has accordingly been little noticed by the critics. My quotations may, I think, suggest that it has a wider range, and subtler variations, than have been commonly observed.

MODERNITY

I suppose every reader of Jane Austen who is familiar with the novels of Fanny Burney or Maria Edgeworth is struck by her surprising air of modernity. It is a quality that she shares with other great imaginative writers. Her modernity is like Chaucer's or Shakespeare's, the effect of her truth. When we say that Shakespeare is of all time, we mean that human nature is of all time and that Shakespeare has told the truth about it. Lesser writers seem more remote because to the distance of time, to differences of manners and language, they add a false distance that comes of imperfect vision and inadequate powers of interpretation. The greatest painters of manners seem to be above their age not because they conceal its idiosyncrasies by abstraction but because, though the manners of one age are very like those of another, only the greatest writers can transcribe them correctly.

Literary fame, though it is sometimes bestowed, and though we pretend that it is maintained, by popular suffrage, is really in the custody of a professional minority. The classics are classical not because they are widely or voluntarily read, but because it is known—from academic curricula, from histories of literature, from the labours of editors—that they deserve homage. One effect of this is to obscure the existence of minor literature in the past, and to produce the illusion that our ancestors, unlike our contemporaries, preferred good books to worse books.

But this hardly holds of a handful of the very greatest writers. Superlative excellence keeps its place in popular esteem by its own equilibrium, and needs no buttress. The popularity of Shakespeare is, indeed, often exaggerated. George III remarked that much of Shakespeare 'is sad stuff; only we mustn't say so'. In fact, not many people are familiar with *Titus Andronicus* or *Henry the Sixth*. But the best plays may, with pardonable hyperbole, be said to have a universal appeal. That is true also of Jane Austen and of Dickens, perhaps of Trollope; but of what other novelists or playwrights who have been dead fifty years?

APPENDIX: THE PORTRAITS

In what follows I am indebted to the expert advice of Sir Henry Hake and Mr. C. K. Adams of the National Portrait Gallery.

I. On 3 May 1948 Messrs. Sotheby offered for sale (lot 265) a 'Pencil Sketch . . . the face and hair in water-colours, of Jane Austen, in a blue paper wrapper inscribed "Cassandra's sketch of Jane, from which a picture was drawn by Mr. Andrews of Maidenhead to be engraved for the Memoir"'.[1] The ultimate provenance of this, as of the letters and other manuscripts of J.A. in the sale, was the collection once in the possession of Charles Austen's granddaughters; this collection, when I first came to know it, had already been denuded of the manuscripts and other relics included in this sale; the residue is described in my edition of the *Memoir*, 1926, pp. xi, xv. The Portrait was bought by the National Portrait Gallery.

Cassandra's sketch had been reproduced in the Hubbacks' *Sailor Brothers*, 1906, 226, where it was slightly embellished by the blockmaker, but was uncoloured.

This disappointing scratch, for it is hardly more, is the only delineation of Jane Austen's *features* (but see No. III below) that can claim authenticity, unless the pretensions of my No. IV should be admitted. When in 1869 J. E. Austen Leigh collected materials for the *Memoir*, it was all he had. The ladies whom he consulted (see above, p. 140) gave Mr. Andrews's recon-

[1] The 'picture' is preserved in the family.

struction very guarded and qualified approval: it was not positively inconsistent with their youthful recollections; perhaps it gave some idea of the truth. It is probably not significant of misgiving that it was omitted from the second edition, since most of the other illustrations of 1870 were suppressed in 1871. The portrait was restored in later editions, and has become tediously familiar.

II. A 'portrait of Jane Austen the Novelist by Zoffany' was reproduced by Lord Brabourne in 1884 and (having been cleaned in the interval) in the *Life* of 1912. It had a pedigree (see *Life*, 63) that any layman might think watertight; but it cannot be Jane Austen. It is a portrait of a young girl which can be dated by the costume to about 1805 (when J.A. was thirty) or later.

III. In my edition of the *Letters* I reproduced, and made bold to describe as a portrait of J.A., a tinted drawing of an unnamed lady, signed and dated by Cassandra: 'C.E.A. 1804' (*not* 1794 as I unhappily printed it).

The evidence on which I relied was circumstantial. I have since seen a letter, in the possession of Mr. R. A. Austen Leigh, from Anna Lefroy to J.E.A.L. at Tenby. It is dated 8 August, and the envelope has the postmark 1862. It contains this passage: '*She* was once I think at Tenby—and once they went as far north as Barmouth— I would give a good deal, that is as much as I could afford, for a sketch which Aunt Cassandra made of her in one of their expeditions—sitting down out of doors on a hot day, with her bonnet strings untied.'

This portrait is described by Sotheby's catalogue (3 May 1948, see above) as 'an excellent view of her back and bonnet'. It is more than that; it shows the graceful outline of a seated lady, and has nothing inconsistent with what is known of J.A.'s figure.

IV. In 1944 the National Portrait Gallery acquired volumes 1 and 2 of the second edition (1816) of *Mansfield Park*. The bookseller who sold the book could not trace its history. Pasted in one volume is a silhouette of a woman's head, with the legend, in a hand not identified, 'L'aimable Jane'. There is a certain presumption that 'Jane' is Jane Austen. Who would insert, in a copy of *Mansfield Park*, a portrait of any other Jane than its author? The epithet 'aimable' perhaps corroborates this presumption.

The volumes contain the modern signature or initials of A. E. Oakley. There is a bare possibility that the recovery of the third volume might give a clue.

J. A.'s letter to James Edward of 16 December 1816 ends 'Adieu Amiable'. It might be significant that in the *Memoir* this is printed 'Aimable'.

ADDENDA

I add a few notes that have occurred in the course of proof-reading.

Pages 1, 142. The letters which Cassandra did *not* destroy were in the fullest sense family letters, intended to be read by, or to, all accessible members of the family (including in one case Sacree, the old nursemaid at Godmersham). Cassandra, moreover, though I have rejected the view of her character taken by Mr. Forster and Mr. Nicolson, was not an evocative correspondent. We are assured of her 'habitual reticence' (63) and that 'she rarely admired anyone' (65). Such economy of expression might well check any tendency in her sister to abound in disclosure or in irrelevant digression. The handful of letters to other correspondents is more revealing. The letters to James Edward and Anna, about their early effusions, tell us something of J.A.'s own literary theory and practice; the letters to Fanny Knight tell us a great deal about her views on love and marriage. Three letters written outside the family give a tantalizing glimpse of what we have lost. Of these two are to Martha Lloyd—who was all but a member of the family: the letter of Nov. 1812 (74.1 in my edition), which tells us of the sale of *P.P.*, and an unpublished letter of Feb. 1813, in which J.A. sympathizes with 'the Princess of Wales . . . poor woman . . . because she is a woman, and because I hate her husband'. A third letter was written within a few weeks of Jane's death to a Miss Anne Sharpe, of whom we know very little, though she is Jane's 'dearest Anne'. Jane then thought she was getting better. 'If I live to be an old woman, I must expect to wish I had died now; blessed in the tenderness of such a family, and before I had survived either them or their affection.'

If the secrets of Jane's workshop were ever revealed (which

I doubt) it would be in letters to Henry. But the author of the *Memoir* satisfied himself that none had been kept.

81. We can only guess at Jane Austen's estimation of the relative merits of her books. It is perhaps worth noting that whereas the title-page of *P.P.* mentions *S.S.*, and the title-page of *M.P.* mentions both *S.S.* and *P.P.*, the title-page of *E.* names only *P.P.*, that of *N.A. and P.* only *P.P.* and *M.P.* The omission of *S.S.* and *E.* in the last case was perhaps Henry's choice, and he might be responsible for the title-page of *E.* too.

94. I call attention to the wording of the letter quoted above, 132: 'the really important points of one's existence even in this world'. The phrase 'even in this world' is no more formulary than is Cassandra's 'I presume to hope'.

115. *Politics*. When Henry Tilney took his sister and her friend for a walk, and monopolized the conversation, he found himself alluding to the political situation; 'and from politics it was an easy step to silence'. The exclusion of women from political discussion is one side of the picture; I find a hint of the other in Darcy's failure to understand the neglect of a gentleman's library 'in times like these'. He was thinking of the dangerous doctrines—religious, philosophical, political— then gaining ground, which could be resisted only with the weapon of sound literature.

117, 124. 'Miss Austen, with the sleepless prudence of perfect sovereignty, is never to be tempted beyond the limits of her parlour.' Walter Raleigh, *The English Novel*, 1894, ch. ix.

I once heard Mr. Aldous Huxley complain of Trollope that he showed no interest in anyone with an income of less than £500 a year. The judgement was inaccurate in point of fact. It was also wholly unjust as an inference. A novelist is entitled to fix the limits of his ideal world. A prudent novelist may think it his duty not to stray into regions where his experience is a fallible guide.

196. I find one instructive parallel in Trollope's account, in ch. ix of *Barchester Towers*, of the family of the Hon. and Rev. Vesey Stanhope. Allowing for an element of caricature, the Stanhopes are as convincing as they are entertaining. Trollope thus describes them:

'The great family characteristic of the Stanhopes might probably be said to be heartlessness; but the want of feeling was, in most of them, accompanied by so great an amount of good nature as to make itself but little noticeable to the world.'

He draws, in the same chapter, a finer distinction: 'Though heartless, the Stanhopes were not selfish.' He means, I think, that as a family they were loyal to each other. As much may be said for the Crawfords, uncle, nephew, and niece.

INDEX I: PERSONS, ETC.

Note. The generations of J.A.'s family are distinguished thus:
GEORGE (her father), JAMES (her brother), *Anna* (her niece).

INDEX II: PLACES